THE
CATHOLIC CHURCH
AND CONVERSION

G. K. CHESTERTON

THE
CATHOLIC CHURCH
AND CONVERSION

IGNATIUS PRESS   SAN FRANCISCO

The text was taken from the original edition
published in New York by Macmillan Press, 1926
Published with ecclesiastical approval
© 1926 by The Macmillan Company
(Rights to the G.K.C. text have been renewed)
Reprinted by permission of A. P. Watt, London

Footnotes were prepared by
James J. Thomson, Jr.,
for the edition of this work published in volume three
of The Collected Works of G. K. Chesterton,
© 1990 by Ignatius Press

Photograph of G. K. Chesterton

Cover design by John Herreid

Reprinted in 2006 by Ignatius Press, San Francisco
ISBN 978-1-58617-073-8 (PB)
ISBN 978-1-68149-468-5 (eBook)
Library of Congress Control Number 2005933367
Printed in the United States of America ⊗

CONTENTS

FOREWORD TO THE NEW EDITION

"We do not really want a religion that is right where we are right. What we want is a religion that is right where we are wrong."
— G. K. Chesterton
"The Exception Proves the Rule"
The Catholic Church and Conversion

There are legions of unsuspecting souls who begin reading Chesterton for one reason or another—for his detective fiction or his literary criticism or his prophetic wisdom or simply his dazzling wit—and who have no attraction, no sympathy whatsoever, for the Catholic Church. Anti-Catholic might be too strong a word to describe them, perhaps not. As they read Chesterton, however, something astonishing happens. They slowly start dropping their defenses. They suddenly find themselves cheering for the Church. Then they finally come running, banging on the doors demanding to be let in. I know something about these people. I have met a lot of them.

And I was one of them myself. I know first
hand that Gilbert Keith Chesterton is a maker
of converts and that he is directly responsible
for an untold number of conversions in the
twentieth and twenty-first centuries.

Although I have read this book many times,
I have to say that there were three really dis-
tinctive readings for me. As with any volume
of Chesterton, it was a completely different
book each time I read it, but more so in this
case. The first time I read it, I was not thinking at all about ever becoming a Catholic. The
second time I read it, I was knee-deep in the
process of my conversion. The third time I read
it was after I had been received into the Church.

In all likelihood, you are reading this book
for one of three reasons, each of which reflects
one of my three readings. Perhaps you have
some fondness for Chesterton but have no
interest in his Catholic faith, or perhaps you
are seriously thinking about becoming a Catholic, or perhaps you already are one. The book
is an utterly different book, depending on the
direction from which it is approached. Yet
Chesterton has the amazing ability to please,
to placate and to provoke, no matter what your

perspective is. No matter who you are or where you are, this is still the right book for you. Your path is delicate, it is dangerous, it is delightful. Even as I urge you to proceed, the thing that I myself keep in mind most of all is the danger. One of the most significant observations Chesterton makes in this book is that the potential convert reaches a stage where nothing said by any opponent of the faith will have the least effect, but one wrong word by a Catholic can do a great deal of damage. Sometimes the worst enemies of the Church are its own members. If there are things about the Church that bother you, you will find Chesterton surprisingly sympathetic, but you will also find that he is almost dismissive of certain things that you may think are very important. To balance this, however, he will give prominence to things you have probably overlooked. He will always surprise you, even shock you. He will tell you flat out that most attacks upon tradition are simply stupid. He will make you appreciate those traditions in a new way. Yes, he will make old things new, and new things will look rather old and tired.

This book cannot be considered as classic apologetics. Chesterton does not systematically deal with each Protestant objection to the Catholic faith, though he does manage to deal with many of them, including some that you probably did not know existed. Rather than thrust and parry, his approach is to create what seems to be a whole new world into which you want to enter. What he has really done, however, is simply given you a new set of eyes with which to see *this* world. He has created a much larger view of things, making you realize how small your view was before. The tradition is broad, the objection is narrow. The tradition is true, the fad is a superstition. The tradition is alive, the revolt is dead. Your view, it turns out, was "dull safety"; his is the "dizzy vision of liberty". You can therefore expect to feel wobbly at times.

Since he writes like no one else, you put yourself at his mercy when you read him, and you find yourself thinking in a different way. Although it seems unusual, it also seems right and fitting. Although it seems utterly original, it also seems strangely familiar. He describes the place where you belong, even though you have never been there.

Chesterton expresses concern that in describing conversion, he might give the wrong impression that his own experience is the same as all other converts. Yet, almost all the converts that I know who have read this book have attested to the fact that Chesterton describes their experience almost exactly. Perhaps it is even more surprising that in spite of Chesterton's concerns about being too personal, this book is surprisingly unautobiographical. We really don't get much information here about Chesterton's own path to Rome. For that, we have to read his *Autobiography*, which I suggest we all do.

The other book that is much more personal than this one is *Orthodoxy*. In that classic work of apologetics and pure rhetoric, Chesterton describes how he first came to embrace Christianity. There is no question that *Orthodoxy* is, in many ways, a defense of the Catholic Church, "the wild truth reeling but erect".

He defended the Catholic Church for a long time before joining it. He admitted that he was standing at the door ushering others in without having entered it himself. His friend and philosophical opponent George Bernard Shaw used to make fun of what he called Chesterton's "Roman Catholic hobby". When Chesterton actually did become Catholic in 1922, however, Shaw fired off a letter saying "Gilbert! This is going too far!"

One of the people who played a key role in Chesterton's conversion was Fr. John O'Connor, the priest who was the inspiration for Chesterton's legendary detective, Father Brown. Also in this cast of characters was Chesterton's friend Maurice Baring, author and diplomat, who was himself a convert; Chesterton's brother Cecil, who died while serving as a soldier in World War I, after having been received into the Church; and Msgr. Ronald Knox, who ironically converted to Catholicism before Chesterton, but did so because of reading Chesterton, and who then served as his spiritual advisor in the days leading up to Chesterton's reception into the Church. It must be mentioned that Chesterton's great friend and fellow Catholic apologist Hilaire Belloc is surprisingly not on this list and in fact was shocked when Chesterton became Catholic. He never thought it would happen. Afterwards, however, he was only too happy to write the original Foreword to this book.

In the *Catholic Church and Conversion*, you will find (and underline) many striking, fundamental and prophetic truths. Perhaps the most prophetic is that the faith will be revived by a new generation after an older generation has neglected it. We sing "Faith of Our Fathers", but Chesterton suggests that it might be more accurate to sing "Faith of Our Children". We are seeing it happening right now. There is a revival in the Catholic Church. It is coming in a large part from the young people.

It is also coming, in some small part, from converts.

In not quite perfect symmetry to each of my three readings, Chesterton describes three stages of conversion: the first is being fair to the Catholic Church, which is impossible; the second is discovering the Catholic Church, which is irresistible; the third is running away from the Catholic Church, which is almost laughable. I say "laughable" because at that point the reasons for holding back can hardly be taken seriously. I say "almost" for one's soul still hangs in the balance. But let me warn anyone who has not yet reached that third stage: the first stage is usually fatal. As soon as you stop being against the Catholic Church, you find yourself being oddly in favor of it. There is no in-between. There is no neutral ground.

At the end, at that third stage, when, as a certain alien life form once said, resistance is futile, there is no more need of convincing; there is only deciding. The intellect is satisfied; the will remains stubborn. There are no more doubts; there is only the pride of a man who refuses to admit he has been wrong about the Roman Catholic Church for a long time. I have often said that my conversion was for me, a glorious defeat. We converts enter the Church with our heads bowed, with a humble spirit we never imagined possible, and then our faith and our hope and our love are rewarded with a blessed and beautiful realization that the Church is larger on the inside than it is on the outside.

—Dale Ahlquist
May 2006

FOREWORD

It is with diffidence that anyone born into the Faith can approach the tremendous subject of Conversion. Indeed, it is easier for one still quite unacquainted with the Faith to approach that subject than it is for one who has had the advantage of the Faith from childhood. There is at once a sort of impertinence in approaching an experience other than one's own (necessarily more imperfectly grasped), and an ignorance of the matter. Those born into the Faith very often go through an experience of their own parallel to, and in some way resembling, that experience whereby original strangers to the Faith come to see it and to accept it. Those born into the Faith often, I say, go through an experience of scepticism in youth, as the years proceed, and it is still a common phenomenon (though not so often to be observed as it was a lifetime ago) for men of the Catholic culture, acquainted with the Church from childhood, to leave it in early manhood and never to return. But it is

nowadays a still more frequent phenomenon—
and it is to this that I allude—for those to
whom scepticism so strongly appealed in youth
to discover, by an experience of men and of
reality in all its varied forms, that the transcendental truths they had been taught in childhood have the highest claims upon their
matured reason.

This experience of the born Catholic may,
I repeat, be called in a certain sense a phenomenon of conversion. But it differs from
conversion properly so called, which rather sig-
nifies the gradual discovery and acceptance of
the Catholic Church by men and women who
began life with no conception of its existence:
for whom it had been during their formative
years no more than a name, perhaps despised,
and certainly corresponding to no known
reality.

Such men and women converts are perhaps
the chief factors in the increasing vigor of the
Catholic Church in our time. The admiration
which the born Catholic feels for their action
is exactly consonant to that which the Church
in its earlier days showed to the martyrs. For
the word "martyr" means "witness." The

phenomenon of conversion apparent in every class, affecting every type of character, is the great modern *witness* to the truth of the claim of the Faith; to the fact that the Faith is reality, and that in it alone is the repose of reality to be found.

In proportion as men know less and less of the subject, in that proportion do they conceive that the entrants into the City of God are of one type, and in that proportion do they attempt some simple definition of the mind which ultimately accepts Catholicism. They will call it a desire for security; or an attraction of the senses such as is exercised by music or by verse. Or they will ascribe it to that particular sort of weakness (present in many minds) whereby they are easily dominated and changed in mood by the action of another.

A very little experience of typical converts in our time makes nonsense of such theories. Men and women enter by every conceivable gate, after every conceivable process of slow intellectual examination, of shock, of vision, of moral trial and even of merely intellectual process. They enter through the action of expanded experience. Some obtain this through travel, some through a reading of history beyond their fellows, some through personal accidents of life. And not only are the avenues of approach to the Faith infinite in number (though all converging; as must be so, since truth is one and error infinitely divided), but the individual types in whom the process of conversion may be observed differ in every conceivable fashion. When you have predicated of one what emotion or what reasoning process brought him into the fold, and you attempt to apply your predicate exactly to another, you will find a misfit. The cynic enters, and so does the sentimentalist; and the fool enters and so does the wise man; the perpetual questioner and doubter and the man too easily accepting immediate authority—they each enter after his kind. You come across an entry into the Catholic Church undoubtedly due to the spectacle, admiration and imitation of some great character observed. Next day you come across an entry into the Catholic Church out of complete loneliness, and you are astonished to find the convert still ignorant of the great mass of the Catholic effect on character. And yet again, immediately after, you will find a totally different third type, the man who enters not from loneliness, nor from the effect of another mind, but who comes in out of contempt for the insufficiency or the evil by which he has been surrounded.

The Church is the natural home of the Human Spirit.

The truth is that if you seek for an explanation of the phenomenon of conversion under any system which bases that phenomenon on illusion, you arrive at no answer to your question. If you imagine conversion to proceed from this or that or the other erroneous or particular limited and insufficient cause, you will soon discover it to be inexplicable.

There is only one explanation of the phenomenon—a phenomenon always present, but particularly arresting to the educated man outside the Catholic Church in the English-speaking countries—there is only one explanation which will account for the multiplicity of such entries and for the infinitely varied quality of the minds attracted by the great change; and that explanation is that the Catholic Church is reality. If a distant mountain may be mistaken for a cloud by many, but is recognised for a stable part of the world (its outline fixed and its quality permanent) by every sort of observer, and among these especially by men famous for their interest in the debate, for their acuteness of vision and for their earlier doubts, the overwhelming presumption is that the thing seen is a piece of objective reality. Fifty men on shipboard strain their eyes for land. Five, then ten, then twenty, make the land-fall and recognise it and establish it for their fellows. To the remainder, who see it not or who think it a bank of fog, there is replied the detail of the outline, the character of the points recognised, and that by the most varied and therefore convergent and convincing witnesses—by some who do not desire that land should be there at all, by some who dread its approach, as well as those who are glad to find it, by some who have long most ridiculed the idea that it was land at all—and it is in this convergence of witnesses that we have one out of the innumerable proofs upon which the rational basis of our religion reposes.

—Hilaire Belloc

I

INTRODUCTORY: A NEW RELIGION

The Catholic faith used to be called the Old
Religion; but at the present moment it has a rec-
ognized place among the New Religions. This
has nothing to do with its truth or falsehood;
but it is a fact that has a great deal to do with
the understanding of the modern world.

It would be very undesirable that modern
men should accept Catholicism merely as a novelty; but it is a novelty. It does act upon its
existing environment with the peculiar force
and freshness of a novelty. Even those who
denounce it generally denounce it as a novelty; as an innovation and not merely a survival. They talk of the "advanced" party in the
Church of England; they talk of the "aggres-
sion" of the Church of Rome. When they talk
of an Extremist they are as likely to mean a
Ritualist as a Socialist. Given any normal

respectable Protestant family, Anglican or Puritan, in England or America, we shall find that Catholicism is actually for practical purposes treated as a new religion, that is, a revolution. It is not a survival. It is not in that sense an antiquity. It does not necessarily owe anything to tradition. In places where tradition can do nothing for it, in places where all the tradition is against it, it is intruding on its own merits; not as a tradition but a truth. The father of some such Anglican or American Puritan family will find, very often, that all his children are breaking away from his own more or less Christian compromise (regarded as normal in the nineteenth century) and going off in various directions after various faiths or fashions which he would call fads. One of his sons will become a Socialist and hang up a portrait of Lenin; one of his daughters will become a Spiritualist and play with a planchette; another daughter will go over to Christian Science and it is quite likely that another son will go over to Rome. The point is, for the moment, that from the point of view of the father, and even in a sense of the family, all these things act after the manner of new religions, of great movements, of enthusiasms that carry young people off their feet and leave older people bewildered or annoyed. Catholicism indeed, even more than the others, is often spoken of as if it were actually one of the wild passions of youth. Optimistic aunts and uncles say that the youth will "get over it," as if it were a childish love affair or that unfortunate business with the barmaid. Darker and sterner aunts and uncles, perhaps at a rather earlier period, used actually to talk about it as an indecent indulgence, as if its literature were literally a sort of pornography. Newman remarks quite naturally, as if there were nothing odd about it at the time, that an undergraduate found with an ascetic manual or a book of monastic meditations was under a sort of cloud or taint, as having been caught with "a bad book" in his possession. He had been wallowing in the sensual pleasure of Nones or inflaming his lusts by contemplating an incorrect number of candles. It is perhaps no longer the custom to regard conversion as a form of dissipation; but it is still common to regard conversion as a form of revolt. And as regards the established convention of much of the modern world, it is a revolt. The worthy merchant of the middle class, the worthy farmer of the

Middle West, when he sends his son to college, does now feel a faint alarm lest the boy should fall among thieves, in the sense of Communists; but he has the same sort of fear lest he should fall among Catholics.

Now he has no fear lest he should fall among Calvinists. He has no fear that his children will become seventeenth-century Supralapsarians,[1] however much he may dislike that doctrine. He is not even particularly troubled by the possibility of their adopting the extreme solfidian[2] conceptions once common among some of the more extravagant Methodists. He is not likely to await with terror the telegram that will inform him that his son has become a Fifth-Monarchy man,[3] any more than that he has joined the Albigensians.[4] He does not exactly lie awake at night wondering whether

[1] Supralapsarianism is a variety of Calvinist predestinarianism that decreed both election and reprobation before (*supra*) the fall (*lapsus*).

[2] Solfidianism is the doctrine of justification by faith alone (*sola fide*); it totally excludes merit and good works.

[3] The Fifth-Monarchy men were Puritan radicals who flourished during the English Civil War of the 1640s. They believed that Christ would return soon to establish his reign on earth, the "Fifth Monarchy".

[4] Albigensianism, a form of Manichaean dualism, arose in southern France in the late twelfth century. In 1208 Pope Innocent III called for a crusade to stamp out the heresy; the orthodox forces prevailed by the 1220s.

Tom at Oxford has become a Lutheran any more than a Lollard.[5] All these religions he dimly recognises as dead religions; or at any rate as old religions. And he is only frightened of new religions. He is only frightened of those fresh, provocative, paradoxical new notions that fly to the young people's heads. But amongst these dangerous juvenile attractions he does in practice class the freshness and novelty of Rome.

Now this is rather odd; because Rome is not so very new. Among these annoying new religions, one is rather an old religion; but it is the only old religion that is so new. When it was originally and really new, no doubt a Roman father often found himself in the same position as the Anglican or Puritan father. He too might find all his children going strange ways and deserting the household gods and the sacred temple of the Capitol. He too might find that one of those children had joined the Christians in their Ecclesia and possibly in their Catacombs. But he would have found that, of

[5] Lollardy developed in fourteenth-century England from the teachings of John Wyclif (c. 1320–1384), whose anti-clericalism and criticism of the Church's wealth and temporal power anticipated ideas that would emerge fully in the Reformation.

his other children, one cared for nothing but the Mysteries of Orpheus, another was inclined to follow Mithras, another was a Neo-Pythagorean who had learned vegetarianism from the Hindoos, and so on. Though the Roman father, unlike the Victorian father, might have the pleasure of exercising the *patria potestas*[6] and cutting off the heads of all the heretics, he could not cut off the stream of all the heresies. Only by this time most of the streams have run rather dry. It is now seldom necessary for the anxious parent to warn his children against the undesirable society of the Bull of Mithras, or even to wean him from the exclusive contemplation of Orpheus; and though we have vegetarians always with us, they mostly know more about proteids than about Pythagoras. But that other youthful extravagance is still youthful. That other new religion is once again new. That one fleeting fashion has refused to fleet; and that ancient bit of modernity is still modern. It is still to the Protestant parent now exactly what it was to the pagan parent then. We might say simply

[6] In ancient Rome, *patria potestas* was the father's absolute authority over members of his household.

that it is a nuisance; but anyhow it is a novelty. It is not simply what the father is used to, or even what the son is used to. It is coming in as something fresh and disturbing, whether as it came to the Greeks who were always seeking some new thing, or as it came to the shepherds who first heard the cry upon the hills of the good news that our language calls the Gospel. We can explain the fact of the Greeks in the time of St. Paul regarding it as a new thing, because it was a new thing. But who will explain why it is still as new to the last of the converts as it was to the first of the shepherds? It is as if a man a hundred years old entered the Olympian games among the young Greek athletes; which would surely have been the basis of a Greek legend. There is something almost as legendary about the religion that is two thousand years old now appearing as a rival of the new religions. That is what has to be explained and cannot be explained away; nothing can turn the legend into a myth. We have seen with our own eyes and heard with our own ears this great modern quarrel between young Catholics and old Protestants; and it is the first step to recognise in any study of modern conversion.

I am not going to talk about numbers and statistics, though I may say something about them later. The first fact to realise is a difference of substance which falsifies all the difference of size. The great majority of Protestant bodies to-day, whether they are strong or weak, are not strengthened in this particular fashion; by the actual attraction of their new followers to their old doctrines. A young man will suddenly become a Catholic priest, or even a Catholic monk, because he has a spontaneous and even impatient personal enthusiasm for the doctrine of Virginity as it appeared to St. Catherine or St. Clare. But how many men become Baptist ministers because they have a personal horror of the idea of an innocent infant coming unconsciously to Christ? How many honest Presbyterian ministers in Scotland really want to go back to John Knox, as a Catholic mystic might want to go back to John of the Cross? These men inherit positions which they feel they can hold with reasonable consistency and general agreement; but they do inherit them. For them religion is tradition. We Catholics naturally do not sneer at tradition; but we say that in this case it is really tradition and nothing else. Not one man in a hundred of these people would ever have joined his present communion if he had been born outside it. Not one man in a thousand of them would have invented anything like his church formulas if they had not been laid down for him. None of them has any real reason for being in their own particular church, whatever good reason they may still have for being outside ours. In other words, the old creed of their communion has ceased to function as a fresh and stimulating idea. It is at best a motto or a war cry and at the worst a catchword. But it is not meeting contemporary ideas like a contemporary idea. In their time and in their turn we believe that those other contemporary ideas will also prove their mortality by having also become mottoes and catchwords and traditions. A century or two hence Spiritualism may be a tradition and Socialism may be a tradition and Christian Science may be a tradition. But Catholicism will not be a tradition. It will still be a nuisance and a new and dangerous thing.

These are the general considerations which govern any personal study of conversion to the Catholic faith. The Church has defended tradition in a time which stupidly denied and despised tradition. But that is simply because the Church is always the only thing defending whatever is at the moment stupidly despised. It is already beginning to appear as the only champion of reason in the twentieth century, as it was the only champion of tradition in the nineteenth. We know that the higher mathematics is trying to deny that two and two make four and the higher mysticism to imagine something that is beyond good and evil. Amid all these antirational philosophies, ours will remain the only rational philosophy. In the same spirit the Church did indeed point out the value of tradition to a time which treated it as quite valueless. The nineteenth-century neglect of tradition and mania for mere documents were altogether nonsensical. They amounted to saying that men always tell lies to children but men never make mistakes in books. But though our sympathies are traditional because they are human, it is not that part of the thing which stamps it as divine. The mark of the Faith is not tradition; it is conversion. It is the miracle by which men find truth in spite of tradition and often with the rending of all the roots of humanity.

It is with the nature of this process that I propose to deal; and it is difficult to deal with it without introducing something of a personal element. My own is only a very trivial case but naturally it is the case I know best; and I shall be compelled in the pages that follow to take many illustrations from it. I have therefore thought it well to put first this general note on the nature of the movement in my time; to show that I am well aware that it is a very much larger and even a very much later movement than is implied in describing my own life or generation. I believe it will be more and more an issue for the rising generation and for the generation after that, as they discover the actual alternative in the awful actualities of our time. And Catholics when they stand up together and sing "Faith of our Fathers" may realise almost with amusement that they might well be singing "Faith of our Children." And in many cases the return has been so recent as almost to deserve the description of a Children's Crusade.

II

THE OBVIOUS BLUNDERS

I have noted that Catholicism really is in the twentieth century what it was in the second century; it is the New Religion. Indeed its very antiquity preserves an attitude of novelty. I have always thought it striking and even stirring that in the venerable invocation of the "Tantum Ergo," which for us seems to come loaded with accumulated ages, there is still the language of innovation; of the antique document that must yield to a new rite. For us the hymn is something of an antique document itself. But the rite is always new.

But if a convert is to write of conversion he must try to retrace his steps out of that shrine back into that ultimate wilderness where he once really believed that this eternal youth was only the "Old Religion." It is a thing exceedingly difficult to do and not often done well, and I for one have little hope of doing it even tolerably well. The difficulty was expressed to me by another convert who said, "I cannot explain why I am a Catholic; because now that I am a Catholic I cannot imagine myself as anything else." Nevertheless, it is right to make the imaginative effort. It is not bigotry to be certain we are right; but it is bigotry to be unable to imagine how we might possibly have gone wrong. It is my duty to try to understand what H. G. Wells can possibly mean when he says that the mediæval Church did not care for education but only for imposing dogmas; it is my duty to speculate (however darkly) on what can have made an intelligent man like Arnold Bennett[7] stone-blind to all the plainest facts about Spain; it is my duty to find if I can the thread of connected thought in George Moore's[8] various condemnations of Catholic Ireland; and it is equally my duty to labour till I understand the strange mental state of G. K. Chesterton when he really assumed that the

[7]Arnold Bennett (1867–1931) was an English novelist, journalist and playwright.

[8]George Moore (1852–1933) was an Irish novelist who contributed to the Irish literary flowering of the early twentieth century.

Catholic Church was a sort of ruined abbey, almost as deserted as Stonehenge.

I must say first that, in my own case, it was at worst a matter of slights rather than slanders. Many converts far more important than I have had to wrestle with a hundred devils of howling falsehood; with a swarm of lies and libels. I owe it to the liberal and Universalist atmosphere of my family, of Stopford Brooke[9] and the Unitarian preachers they followed, that I was always just sufficiently enlightened to be out of the reach of Maria Monk.[10] Nevertheless, as this is but a private privilege for which I have to be thankful, it is necessary to say something of what I might be tempted to call the obvious slanders, but that better men than I have not always seen that the slander was obvious. I do not think that they exercise much influence on the generation that is younger than mine. The worst temptation of the most pagan

[9] Stopford Brooke (1832–1916), a prominent Anglican preacher in Ireland, repudiated his church in 1880 because he could no longer accept its teachings.

[10] In 1836 Maria Monk, claiming to have escaped from a convent in Montreal, published the salacious *Awful Disclosures of Maria Monk*. Although her tale was quickly exposed as a hoax, the book became a standard weapon used by anti-Catholics.

youth is not so much to denounce monks for breaking their vow as to wonder at them for keeping it. But there is a state of transition that must be allowed for in which a vague Protestant prejudice would rather like to have it both ways. There is still a sort of woolly-minded philistine who would be content to consider a friar a knave for his unchastity and a fool for his chastity. In other words, these dying calumnies are dying but not dead; and there are still enough people who may still be held back by such crude and clumsy obstacles that it is necessary to some extent to clear them away. After that we can consider what may be called the real obstacles, the real difficulties we find, which, as a fact, are generally the very opposite of the difficulties we are told about. But let us consider the evidence of all these things being black, before we go on to the inconvenient fact of their being white.

The usual protest of the Protestant, that the Church of Rome is afraid of the Bible, did not, as I shall explain in a moment, have any great terrors for me at any time. This was by no merit of my own, but by the accident of my age and situation. For I grew up in a world in which the Protestants, who had just proved that Rome did not believe the Bible, were excitedly discovering that they did not believe the Bible themselves. Some of them even tried to combine the two condemnations and say that they were steps of progress. The next step in progress consisted in a man kicking his father for having locked up a book of such beauty and value, a book which the son then proceeded to tear into a thousand pieces. I early discovered that progress is worse than Protestantism so far as stupidity is concerned. But most of the free-thinkers who were friends of mine happened to think sufficiently freely to see that the Higher Criticism was much more of an attack on Protestant Bible-worship than on Roman authority. Anyhow, my family and friends were more concerned with the opening of the book of Darwin than the book of Daniel; and most of them regarded the Hebrew Scriptures as if they were Hittite sculptures. But, even then, it would seem odd to worship the sculptures as gods and then smash them as idols and still go on blaming somebody else for not having worshipped them enough. But here again it is hard for me to know how far my own experience is representative, or whether it would not be well to say more of these purely Protestant prejudices and doubts than I, from my own experience, am able to say.

The Church is a house with a hundred gates; and no two men enter at exactly the same angle. Mine was at least as much Agnostic as Anglican, though I accepted for a time the borderland of Anglicanism; but only on the assumption that it could really be Anglo-Catholicism. There is a distinction of ultimate intention there which in the vague English atmosphere is often missed. It is not a difference of degree but of definite aim. There are High Churchmen as much as Low Churchmen who are concerned first and last to save the Church of England. Some of them think it can be saved by calling it Catholic, or making it Catholic, or believing that it is Catholic; but *that* is what they want to save. But I did not start out with the idea of saving the English Church, but of finding the Catholic Church. If the two were one, so much the better; but I had never conceived of Catholicism as a sort of showy attribute or attraction to be tacked on to my own national body, but as

the inmost soul of the true body, wherever
it might be. It might be said that Anglo-
Catholicism was simply my own uncompleted
conversion to Catholicism. But it was from a
position originally much more detached and
indefinite that I had been converted, an atmosphere if not agnostic at least pantheistic or unitarian. To this I owe the fact that I find it very
difficult to take some of the Protestant prop-
ositions even seriously. What is any man who
has been in the real outer world, for instance,
to make of the everlasting cry that Catholic
traditions are condemned by the Bible? It indi-
cates a jumble of topsy-turvy tests and tail-
foremost arguments, of which I never could at
any time see the sense. The ordinary sensible
sceptic or pagan is standing in the street (in
the supreme character of the man in the street)
and he sees a procession go by of the priests
of some strange cult, carrying their object of
worship under a canopy, some of them wear-
ing high head-dresses and carrying symbolical
staffs, others carrying scrolls and sacred records,
others carrying sacred images and lighted candles before them, others sacred relics in caskets
or cases, and so on. I can understand the

spectator saying, "This is all hocus-pocus"; I
can even understand him, in moments of irritation, breaking up the procession, throwing
down the images, tearing up the scrolls, dancing on the priests and anything else that might
express that general view. I can understand his
saying, "Your croziers are bosh, your candles
are bosh, your statues and scrolls and relics and
all the rest of it are bosh." But in what conceivable frame of mind does he rush in to select
one particular scroll of the scriptures of this
one particular group (a scroll which had always
belonged to them and been a part of their
hocus-pocus, if it was hocus-pocus); why in
the world should the man in the street say that
one particular scroll was *not* bosh, but was the
one and only truth by which all the other things
were to be condemned? Why should it not be
as superstitious to worship the scrolls as the
statues, of that one particular procession? Why
should it not be as reasonable to preserve the
statues as the scrolls, by the tenets of that particular creed? To say to the priests, "Your statues and scrolls are condemned by our common
sense," is sensible. To say, "Your statues are condemned by your scrolls, and we are going to

worship one part of your procession and wreck the rest," is not sensible from any standpoint, least of all that of the man in the street.

Similarly, I could never take seriously the fear of the priest, as of something unnatural and unholy; a dangerous man in the home. Why should a man who wanted to be wicked encumber himself with special and elaborate promises to be good? There might sometimes be a reason for a priest being a profligate. But what was the reason for a profligate being a priest? There are many more lucrative walks of life in which a person with such shining talents for vice and villainy might have made a brighter use of his gifts. Why should a man encumber himself with vows that nobody could expect him to take and he did not himself expect to keep? Would any man make himself poor in order that he might become avaricious; or take a vow of chastity frightfully difficult to keep in order to get into a little more trouble when he did not keep it? All that early and sensational picture of the sins of Rome always seemed to me silly even when I was a boy or an unbeliever; and I cannot describe how I passed out of it because I was never in it. I remember asking some friends at

Cambridge, people of the Puritan tradition, why in the world they were so afraid of Papists; why a priest in somebody's house was a peril or an Irish servant the beginning of a pestilence. I asked them why they could not simply disagree with Papists and say so, as they did with Theosophists[11] or Anarchists. They seemed at once pleased and shocked with my daring, as if I had undertaken to convert a burglar or tame a mad dog. Perhaps their alarm was really wiser than my bravado. Anyhow, I had not then the most shadowy notion that the burglar would convert me. That, however, I am inclined to think, is the subconscious intuition in the whole business. It must either mean that they suspect that our religion has something about it so wrong that the hint of it is bad for anybody; or else that it has something so right that the presence of it would convert anybody. To do them justice, I think most of them darkly suspect the second and not the first.

A shade more plausible than the notion that Popish priests merely seek after evil was the

---

[11] Theosophy, a syncretistic faith that combined elements from Christianity and various Asian religions, was founded in New York City in 1875 by Helena Blavatsky.

notion that they are exceptionally ready to seek good by means of evil. In vulgar language, it is the notion that if they are not sensual they are always sly. To dissipate this is a mere matter of experience; but before I had any experience I had seen some objections to the thing even in theory. The theory attributed to the Jesuits was very often almost identical with the practice adopted by nearly everybody I knew. Everybody in society practised verbal economies, equivocations and often direct fictions, without any sense of essential falsehood. Every gentleman was expected to say he would be delighted to dine with a bore; every lady said that somebody else's baby was beautiful if she thought it as ugly as sin; for they did not think it a sin to avoid saying ugly things. This might be right or wrong; but it was absurd to pillory half a dozen Popish priests for a crime committed daily by half a million Protestant laymen. The only difference was that the Jesuits had been worried enough about the matter to try to make rules and limitations saving as much verbal veracity as possible; whereas the happy Protestants were not worried about it at all, but told lies from morning to night as merrily and innocently as the birds sing in the trees. The fact is, of course, that the modern world is full of an utterly lawless casuistry because the Jesuits were prevented from making a lawful casuistry. But every man is a casuist or a lunatic.

It is true that this general truth was hidden from many by certain definite assertions. I can only call them, in simple language, Protestant lies about Catholic lying. The men who repeated them were not necessarily lying, because they were repeating. But the statements were of the same lucid and precise order as a statement that the Pope has three legs or that Rome is situated at the North Pole. There is no more doubt about their nature than that. One of them, for instance, is the positive statement, once heard everywhere and still heard often: "Roman Catholics are taught that anything is lawful if done for the good of the Church." This is not the fact; and there is an end of it. It refers to a definite statement of an institution whose statements are very definite; and it can be proved to be totally false. Here as always the critics cannot see that they are trying to have it both ways. They are always complaining that our creed is cut and dried; that we are told what to believe and must believe nothing else; that it is all written down for us in bulls and confessions of faith. In so far as this is true, it brings a matter like this to the point of legal and literal truth, which can be tested; and so tested, it is a lie. But even here I was saved at a very early stage by noticing a curious fact. I noticed that those who were most ready to blame priests for relying on rigid formulas seldom took the trouble to find out what the formulas were. I happened to pick up some of the amusing pamphlets of James Britten, as I might have picked up any other pamphlets of any other propaganda; but they set me on the track of that delightful branch of literature which he called Protestant Fiction. I found some of that fiction on my own account, dipping into novels by Joseph Hocking[12] and others. I am only concerned with them here to illustrate this particular and curious fact about exactitude. I could not understand why these romancers never took the trouble to find out a few elementary facts

[12] Joseph Hocking (1860–1937) was an English novelist and preacher in the United Methodist Free Church.

about the thing they denounced. The facts might easily have helped the denunciation, where the fictions discredited it. There were any number of real Catholic doctrines I should then have thought disgraceful to the Church. There are any number which I can still easily imagine being made to look disgraceful to the Church. But the enemies of the Church never found these real rocks of offence. They never looked for them. They never looked for anything. They seemed to have simply made up out of their own heads a number of phrases, such as a Scarlet Woman of deficient intellect might be supposed to launch on the world; and left it at that. Boundless freedom reigned; it was not treated as if it were a question of fact at all. A priest might say anything about the Faith; because a Protestant might say anything about the priest. These novels were padded with pronouncements like this one, for instance, which I happen to remember: "Disobeying a priest is the one sin for which there is no absolution. We term it a reserved case." Now obviously a man writing like that is simply imagining what might exist; it has never occurred to him to go and ask if it does exist.

He has heard the phrase "a reserved case" and considers, in a poetic reverie, what he shall make it mean. He does not go and ask the nearest priest what it does mean. He does not look it up in an encyclopædia or any ordinary work of reference. There is no doubt about the fact that it simply means a case reserved for ecclesiastical superiors and not to be settled finally by the priest. That may be a fact to be denounced; but anyhow it is a fact. But the man much prefers to denounce his own fancy. Any manual would tell him that there is no sin "for which there is no absolution"; not disobeying the priest; not assassinating the Pope. It would be easy to find out these facts and quite easy to base a Protestant invective upon them. It puzzled me very much, even at that early stage, to imagine why people bringing controversial charges against a powerful and prominent institution should thus neglect to test their own case, and should draw in this random way on their own imagination. It did not make me any more inclined to be a Catholic; in those days the very idea of such a thing would have seemed crazy. But it did save me from swallowing all the solid and solemn

assertion about what Jesuits said and did. I did
not accept quite so completely as others the
well-ascertained and widely accepted fact that
"Roman Catholics may do anything for the
good of the Church"; because I had already
learned to smile at equally accepted truths like
"Disobeying a priest is the one sin for which
there is no absolution." I never dreamed that
the Roman religion was true; but I knew that
its accusers, for some reason or other, were curi-
ously inaccurate.

It is strange to me to go back to these things
now, and to think that I ever took them even
as seriously as that. But I was not very serious
even then; and certainly I was not serious long.
The last lingering shadow of the Jesuit, glid-
ing behind curtains and concealing himself in
cupboards, faded from my young life about the
time when I first caught a distant glimpse of
the late Father Bernard Vaughan.[13] He was the
only Jesuit I ever knew in those days; and as
you could generally hear him half a mile away,
he seemed to be ill-selected for the duties of a

[13] Father Bernard Vaughan (1847–1922) was an English Jesuit famed
for his preaching and his work among the poor in Manchester and
London.

curtain-glider. It has always struck me as curious that this Jesuit raised a storm by refusing to be Jesuitical (in the journalese sense I mean), by refusing to substitute smooth equivocation and verbal evasion for a brute fact. Because he talked about "killing Germans" when Germans had to be killed, all our shifty and shamefaced morality was shocked at him. And none of those protesting Protestants took thought for a moment to realise that they were showing all the shuffling insincerity they attributed to the Jesuits, and the Jesuit was showing all the plain candour that they claimed for the Protestant.

I could give a great many other instances besides these I have given of the hidden Bible, the profligate priest or the treacherous Jesuit. I could go steadily through the list of all these more old-fashioned charges against Rome and show how they affected me, or rather why they did not affect me. But my only purpose here is to point out, as a preliminary, that they did not affect me at all. I had all the difficulties that a heathen would have had in becoming a Catholic in the fourth century. I had very few of the difficulties that a Protestant had, from

the seventeenth to the nineteenth. And I owe
this to men whose memories I shall always hon-
our; to my father and his circle and the literary tradition of men like George Macdonald[14]
and the Universalists of the Victorian Age. If I
was born on the wrong side of the Roman
wall, at least I was not born on the wrong side
of the No Popery quarrel; and if I did not
inherit a fully civilised faith, neither did I inherit
a barbarian feud. The people I was born
amongst wished to be just to Catholics if they
did not always understand them; and I should
be very thankless if I did not record of them
that (like a very much more valuable convert)
I can say I was born free.

I will add one example to illustrate this
point, because it leads us on to larger matters.
After a long time—I might almost say after a
lifetime—I have at last begun to realise what
the worthy Liberal or Socialist of Balham or
Battersea really means when he says he is an
Internationalist and that humanity should be
preferred to the narrowness of nations. It
dawned on me quite suddenly, after I had talked

---

[14] George Macdonald (1824–1905) was a Scottish poet and novelist.

to such a man for many hours, that of course
he had really been brought up to believe that
God's Englishmen were the Chosen Race. Very
likely his father or uncle actually thought they
were the lost Ten Tribes. Anyhow, everything
from his daily paper to his weekly sermon
assumed that they were the salt of the earth,
and especially that they were the salt of the
sea. His people had never thought outside their
British nationality. They lived in an Empire on
which the sun never set, or possibly never rose.
Their Church was emphatically the Church of
England—even if it was a chapel. Their religion was the Bible that went everywhere with
the Union Jack. And when I realised that, I
realised the whole story. That was why they
were excited by the exceedingly dull theory
of the Internationalist. That was why the brotherhood of nations, which to me was a truism,
to them was a trumpet. That was why it seemed
such a thrilling paradox to say that we must
love foreigners; it had in it the divine paradox
that we must love enemies. That was why the
Internationalist was always planning deputa-
tions and visits to foreign capitals and heart-
to-heart talks and hands across the sea. It was

the marvel of discovering that foreigners had hands, let alone hearts. There was in that excitement a sort of stifled cry: "Look! Frenchmen also have two legs! See! Germans have noses in the same place as we!" Now a Catholic, especially a born Catholic, can never understand that attitude, because from the first his whole religion is rooted in the unity of the race of Adam, the one and only Chosen Race. He is loyal to his own country; indeed he is generally ardently loyal to it, such local affections being in other ways very natural to his religious life, with its shrines and relics. But just as the relic follows upon the religion, so the local loyalty follows on the universal brotherhood of all men. The Catholic says, "Of course we must love all men; but what do all men love? They love their lands, their lawful boundaries, the memories of their fathers. That is the justification of being national, that it is normal." But the Protestant patriot really never thought of any patriotism except his own. In that sense Protestantism is patriotism. But unfortunately it is only patriotism. It starts with it and never gets beyond it. We start with mankind and go beyond it to all the varied loves and traditions of mankind. There never was a more illuminating flash than that which lit up the last moment of one of the most glorious of English Protestants; one of the most Protestant and one of the most English. For that is the meaning of that phrase of Nurse Cavell,[15] herself the noblest martyr of our modern religion of nationality, when the very shaft of the white sun of death shone deep into her mind and she cried aloud, like one who had just discovered something, "I see now that patriotism is not enough."

There was this in common between the Catholics to whom I have come and the Liberals among whom I was born: neither of them would ever have imagined for a moment that patriotism was enough. But that insular idealism by which that great lady lived really had taught her unconsciously from childhood that patriotism *was* enough. Not seldom has the English lady appeared in history as a heroine; but generally as facing and defying strangers or savages, not specially as feeling them as fellows and equals. Those last words of the English

[15] Edith Cavell (1865–1915) was an English nurse executed as a spy by the Germans during World War I.

martyr in Belgium have often been quoted by mere cosmopolitans; but cosmopolitans are the last people really to understand them. *They* are generally trying to prove, not that patriotism is not enough, but that it is a great deal too much. The point is here that hundreds of the most heroic and high-minded people in Protestant countries have really assumed that it is enough to be a patriot. The most careless and cynical of Catholics knows better; and so did the most vague and visionary of Universalists. Of all the Protestant difficulties, which I here find it hard to imagine, this is perhaps the most common and in many ways commendable: the fact that the normal British subject begins by being so very British. By accident I did not. The tradition I heard in my youth, the simple, the too simple truths inherited from Priestly[16] and Martineau,[17] had in them something of that grand generalisation upon men as men which, in the first of those great figures, faced the howling Jingoism

[16] Joseph Priestley (1733–1804) was an English political radical, scientist and key figure in the development of Unitarianism. Chesterton spells the name incorrectly.
[17] James Martineau (1805–1900) was an English philosopher and Unitarian minister.

of the French Wars[18] and defied even the legend of Trafalgar. It is to that tradition that I owe
the fact, whether it be an advantage or a disadvantage, that I cannot worthily analyse the very
heroic virtues of a Plymouth Brother[19] whose
only centre is Plymouth. For that rationalism,
defective as it was, began long ago in the same
central civilisation in which the Church herself
began; if it has ended in the Church it began long
ago in the Republic: in a world where all these
flags and frontiers were unknown; where all
these state establishments and national sects were
unthinkable; a vast cosmopolitan cosmos that had
never heard the name of England, or conceived
the image of a kingdom separate and at war; in
that vast pagan peace which was the matrix of
all these mysteries, which had forgotten the free
cities and had not dreamed of the small nationalities; which knew only humanity, the *humanum
genus*, and the name of Rome.

The Catholic Church loves nations as she
loves men; because they are her children. But

[18] The French Wars were a series of conflicts between England and
France that lasted from 1793 until the defeat of Napoleon in 1815.

[19] The Plymouth Brethren, a millenarian sect, arose in Plymouth, England, in the 1830s.

they certainly are her children, in the sense
that they are secondary to her in time and process of production. This is, as it happens, a
very good example of a fallacy that often con-
fuses discussion about the convert. The same
people who call the convert a pervert, and especially a traitor to patriotism, very often use the
other catchword to the effect that he is forced
to believe this or that. But it is not really a
question of what a man is made to believe but
of what he must believe; what he cannot help
believing. He cannot disbelieve in an elephant
when he has seen one; and he cannot treat the
Church as a child when he has discovered that
she is his mother. She is not only his mother
but his country's mother in being much older
and more aboriginal than his country. She is
such a mother not in sentimental feeling
but in historical fact. He cannot think one thing
when he knows the contrary thing. He
cannot think that Christianity was invented
by Penda of Mercia,[20] who sent missionaries
to the heathen Augustine and the rude and

---

[20] Penda of Mercia was a pagan Anglo-Saxon king of the seventh
century.

barbarous Gregory.[21] He cannot think that the Church first rose in the middle of the British Empire, and not of the Roman Empire. He cannot think that England existed, with cricket and fox-hunting and the Jacobean translation[22] all complete, when Rome was founded or when Christ was born. It is no good talking about his being "free" to believe these things. He is exactly as free to believe them as he is to believe that a horse has feathers or that the sun is pea green. He cannot believe them when once he fully realises them; and among such things is the notion that the national claim upon a good patriot is in its nature more absolute, ancient and authoritative than the claim of the whole religious culture which first mapped out its territories and anointed its kings. That religious culture does indeed encourage him to fight to the last for his country, as for his family. But that is because the religious culture is generous and imaginative and humane and knows that men must

[21] In 596 Pope Gregory I sent Augustine and forty monks to preach the gospel in England. Augustine became the first archbishop of Canterbury, and died in 604.

[22] The Jacobean translation is the King James Version of the Bible, completed in 1611.

have intimate and individual ties. But those secondary loyalties are secondary in time and logic to the law of universal morality which justifies them. And if the patriot is such a fool as to force the issue against that universal tradition from which his own patriotism descends, if he presses his claim to priority over the primitive law of the whole earth—then he will have brought it on himself if he is answered with the pulverising plainness of the Book of Job. As God said to the man, "Where were you when the foundations of the world were laid?" [23] We might well say to the nation, "Where were you when the foundations of the Church were laid?" And the nation will not know in the least what to answer—if it should wish to answer—but will be forced to put its hand upon its mouth, if only like one who yawns and falls asleep.

I have taken this particular case of patriotism because it concerns at least an emotion in which I profoundly believe and happen to feel strongly. I have always done my best to defend it; though I have sometimes become

---

[23] The quotation is from Job 38:4.

suspect by sympathising with other people's patriotism besides my own. But I cannot see how it can be defended except as part of a larger morality; and the Catholic morality happens to be one of the very few large moralities now ready to defend it. But the Church defends it as one of the duties of men and not as the whole duty of man; as it was in the Prussian theory of the State and too often in the British theory of the Empire. And for this the Catholic rests, exactly as the Universalist Unitarian rested, upon the actual fact of a human unity anterior to all these healthy and natural human divisions. But it is absurd to treat the Church as a novel conspiracy attacking the State, when the State was only recently a novel experiment arising within the Church. It is absurd to forget that the Church itself received the first loyalties of men who had not yet even conceived the notion of founding such a national and separate state; that the Faith really was not only the faith of our fathers, but the faith of our fathers before they had even named our fatherland.

III

THE REAL OBSTACLES

In the last chapter I have dealt in a preliminary fashion with the Protestant case in the conventional controversial sense. I have dealt with the objections which I suspected very early of being prejudices and which I now know to be prejudices. I have dealt last and at the greatest length with what I believe to be the noblest of all the prejudices of Protestantism: that which is simply founded on patriotism. I do not think patriotism is necessarily prejudice; but I am quite sure it must be prejudice and nothing else but prejudice, unless it is covered by some common morality. And a patriotism that does not allow other people to be patriots is not a morality but an immorality. Even such a tribal prejudice, however, is a more respectable thing than most of the rags and tatters of stale slander and muddle-headedness which I am obliged to put first as the official policy of the opposition to the Church. These stale stories seem to count for a great deal with people who are resolved to keep far away from the Church. I do not believe they ever counted with anybody who had begun to draw near to it. When a man really sees the Church, even if he dislikes what he sees, he does not see what he had expected to dislike. Even if he wants to slay it he is no longer able to slander it; though he hates it at sight, what he sees is not what he looked to see; in that place he may gain a new passion but he loses his old prejudice. There drops from him the holy armour of his invincible ignorance; he can never be so stupid again. If he has a ready mind he can doubtless set his new reasons in some sort of order and even attempt to link them with his lost tradition. But the thing he hates is there; and the last chapter was wholly devoted to the study of things that are not there.

The real reasons are almost the opposite of the recognised reasons. The real difficulties are almost the opposite of the recognised difficulties. This is connected, of course, with a general fact, now so large and obvious but still not clearly comprehended and confessed. The whole case of Protestantism against Catholicism has been turned clean round and is facing the contrary way. On practically every single point on which the Reformation accused the Church, the modern world has not only acquitted the Church of the crime, but has actually charged it with the opposite crime. It is as if the reformers had mobbed the Pope for being a miser, and then the court had not only acquitted him but had censured him for his extravagance in scattering money among the mob. The principle of modern Protestantism seems to be that so long as we go on shouting "To hell with the Pope" there is room for the widest differences of opinion about whether he should go to the hell of the misers or the hell of the spendthrifts. This is what is meant by a broad basis for Christianity and the statement that there is room for many different opinions side by side. When the reformer says that the principles of the Reformation give freedom to different points of view, he means that they give freedom to the Universalist to curse Rome for having too much predestination and to the Calvinist to curse her for having too little. He means that in that happy family there is a place for the No Popery man who finds Purgatory too tender-hearted and also for the other No Popery man who finds Hell too harsh. He means that the same description can somehow be made to cover the Tol-stoyan who blames priests because they permit patriotism and the Diehard who blames priests because they represent Internationalism. After all, the essential aim of true Christianity is that priests should be blamed; and who are we that we should set narrow dogmatic limits to the various ways in which various temperaments may desire to blame them? Why should we allow a cold difficulty of the logician, technically called a contradiction in terms, to stand between us and the warm and broadening human brotherhood of all who are full of sincere and unaffected dislike of their neighbours? Religion is of the heart, not of the head; and as long as all our hearts are full of a hatred for everything that our fathers loved, we can go on flatly contradicting each other for ever about what there is to be hated.

Such is the larger and more liberal modern attack upon the Church. It is quite inconsistent with the old doctrinal attack; but it does not propose to lose the advantages arising from any sort of attack. But in a somewhat analogous fashion, it will be found that the real difficulties of a modern convert are almost the direct contrary of those which were alleged by the more ancient Protestants. Protestant pamphlets do not touch even remotely any of the real hesitations that he feels; and even Catholic pamphlets have often been concerned too much with answering the Protestant pamphlets. Indeed the only sense in which the priests and propagandists of Catholicism can really be said to be behind the times is that they sometimes go on flogging a dead horse and killing a heresy long after it has killed itself. But even that is, properly understood, a fault on the side of chivalry. The preacher, and even the persecutor, really takes the heresy more seriously than it is seen ultimately to deserve; the inquisitor has more respect for the heresy than the heretics have. Still, it is true that the grounds of suspicion or fear that do really fill the convert, and sometimes paralyse him at the very point of conversion, have really nothing in the world to do with this old crop of crude slanders and fallacies, and are often the very inversion of them.

The short way of putting it is to say that he is no longer afraid of the vices but very much afraid of the virtues of Catholicism. For instance, he has forgotten all about the old nonsense of the cunning lies of the confessional, in his lively and legitimate alarm of the truthfulness of the confessional. He does not recoil from its insincerity but from its sincerity; nor is he necessarily insincere in doing so. Realism is really a rock of offence; it is not at all unnatural to shrink from it; and most modern realists only manage to like it because they are careful to be realistic about other people. He is near enough to the sacrament of penance to have discovered its realism and not near enough to have yet discovered its reasonableness and its common sense. Most of those who have gone through this experience have a certain right to say, like the old soldier to his ignorant comrade, "Yes, I was afraid; and if you were half as much afraid, you would run away." Perhaps it is just as well that people go through this stage before discovering how very little there is to be afraid of. In any case, I will say little more of that example here, having a feeling that absolution, like death and marriage, is a thing that a man ought to find out for himself. It will be enough to say that this is perhaps the supreme example of the fact that the Faith is a paradox that measures more within than without. If that be true of the smallest church, it is truer still of the yet smaller confessional-box, that is like a church within a church. It is almost a good thing that nobody outside should know what gigantic generosity, and even geniality, can be locked up in a box, as the legendary casket held the heart of the giant. It is a satisfaction, and almost a joke, that it is only in a dark corner and a cramped space that any man can discover that mountain of magnanimity.

It is the same with all the other points of attack, especially the old ones. The man who has come so far as that along the road has long left behind him the notion that the priest will force him to abandon his will. But he is not unreasonably dismayed at the extent to which he may have to use his will. He is not frightened because, after taking this drug, he will be henceforward irresponsible. But he is very much frightened because he will be responsible. He will have somebody to be responsible

to and he will know what he is responsible
for; two uncomfortable conditions which his
more fortunate fellow-creatures have nowadays entirely escaped. There are of course many
other examples of the same principle: that there
is indeed an interval of acute doubt, which is,
strictly speaking, rather fear than doubt, since
in some cases at least (as I shall point out else-
where) there is actually least doubt when there
is most fear.

But anyhow, the doubts are hardly ever of
the sort suggested by ordinary anti-Catholic
propaganda; and it is surely time that such propagandists brought themselves more in touch
with the real problem. The Catholic is scarcely
ever frightened of the Protestant picture of
Catholicism; but he is sometimes frightened
of the Catholic picture of Catholicism; which
may be a good reason for not disproportion-
ately stressing the difficult or puzzling parts of
the scheme. For the convert's sake, it should
also be remembered that one foolish word from
inside does more harm than a hundred thousand foolish words from outside. The latter he
has already learned to expect, like a blind hail
or rain beating upon the Ark; but the voices

from within, even the most casual and accidental, he is already prepared to regard as holy or more than human; and though this is unfair to people who only profess to be human beings, it is a fact that Catholics ought to remember. There is many a convert who has reached a stage at which no word from any Protestant or pagan could any longer hold him back. Only the word of a Catholic can keep him from Catholicism.

It is quite false, in my experience, to say that Jesuits, or any other Roman priests, pester and persecute people in order to proselytise. Nobody has any notion of what the whole story is about, who does not know that, through those long and dark and indecisive days, it is the man who persecutes himself. The apparent inaction of the priest may be something like the statuesque stillness of the angler; and such an attitude is not unnatural in the functions of a fisher of men. But it is very seldom impatient or premature and the person acted upon is quite lonely enough to realise that it is nothing merely external that is tugging at his liberty. The laity are probably less wise; for in most communions the ecclesiastical layman is more ecclesiastical than is good for his health, and certainly much more ecclesiastical than the ecclesiastics. My experience is that the amateur is generally much more angry than the professional; and if he expresses his irritation at the slow process of conversion, or the inconsistencies of the intermediate condition, he may do a great deal of harm, of the kind that he least intends to do. I know in my own case that I always experienced a slight setback whenever some irresponsible individual interposed to urge me on. It is worth while, for practical reasons, to testify to such experience, because it may guide the convert when he in his turn begins converting. Our enemies no longer really know how to attack the faith; but that is no reason why we should not know how to defend it.

Yet even that one trivial or incidental caution carries with it a reminder of what has been already noted: I mean the fact that whatever be the Catholic's worries, they are the very contrary of the Protestant's warnings. Merely as a matter of personal experience, I have been led to note here that it is not generally the priest, but much more often the layman, who rather too ostentatiously compasses sea and land

to make one proselyte. All the creepy and
uncanny whispers about the horror of having
the priest in the home, as if he were a sort of
vampire or a monster intrinsically different from
mankind, vanishes with the smallest experience of the militant layman. The priest does
his job, but it is much more his secular co-
religionist who is disposed to explain it and
talk about it. I do not object to laymen pros-
elytising; for I never could see, even when I
was practically a pagan, why a man should not
urge his own opinions if he liked and that opinion as much as any other. I am not likely to
complain of the evangelising energy of Mr.
Hilaire Belloc or Mr. Eric Gill;[24] if only because
I owe to it the most intelligent talks of my
youth. But it is that sort of man who prose-
lytises in that sort of way; and the conventional caricature is wrong again when it always
represents him in a cassock. Catholicism is not
spread by any particular professional tricks or
tones or secret signs or ceremonies. Catholicism is spread by Catholics; but not certainly,

[24]Eric Gill (1882–1940) was an English sculptor, engraver, printer
and spiritual writer who defended craftsmanship against industrial
manufacturing. He converted to Catholicism in 1913.

in private life at least, merely by Catholic priests. I merely give this here out of a hundred examples, as showing once again that the old traditional version of the terrors of Popery was almost always wrong, even where it might possibly have been right. A man may say if he likes that Catholicism is the enemy; and he may be stating from his point of view a profound spiritual truth. But if he says that Clericalism is the enemy, he is repeating a catchword.

It is my experience that the convert commonly passes through three stages or states of mind. The first is when he imagines himself to be entirely detached, or even to be entirely indifferent, but in the old sense of the term, as when the Prayer Book talks of judges who will truly and indifferently administer justice. Some flippant modern person would probably agree that our judges administer justice very indifferently. But the older meaning was legitimate and even logical and it is that which is applicable here. The first phase is that of the young philosopher who feels that he ought to be fair to the Church of Rome. He wishes to do it justice; but chiefly because he sees that it suffers injustice. I remember that when I was first

on the *Daily News*, the great Liberal organ of
the Nonconformists, I took the trouble to draw
up a list of fifteen falsehoods which I found
out, by my own personal knowledge, in a
denunciation of Rome by Messrs. Horton and
Hocking. I noted, for instance, that it was nonsense to say that the Covenanters[25] fought for
religious liberty when the Covenant denounced
religious toleration; that it was false to say the
Church only asked for orthodoxy and was indifferent to morality, since, if this was true of anybody, it was obviously true of the supporters
of salvation by faith and not of salvation by
works; that it was absurd to say that Catholics
introduced a horrible sophistry of saying that
a man might sometimes tell a lie, since every
sane man knows he would tell a lie to save a
child from Chinese torturers; that it missed the
whole point, in this connection, to quote Ward's
phrase,[26] "Make up your mind that you are
justified in lying and then lie like a trooper,"

[25] The Covenanters were Scotsmen who subscribed to the National
Covenant of 1638, which called for the defense of Presbyterianism
against corruption and error.

[26] William George Ward (1812–1882) was an English moral philosopher and participant in the Oxford Movement; he converted to
Catholicism in 1845.

for Ward's argument was against equivocation
or what people call Jesuitry. He meant, "When
the child really is hiding in the cupboard and
the Chinese torturers really are chasing him
with red-hot pincers, then (and then only) be
sure that you are right to deceive and do not
hesitate to lie; but do not stoop to equivocate.
Do not bother yourself to say, 'The child is in
a wooden house not far from here,' meaning
the cupboard; but say the child is in Chiswick
or Chimbora zoo, or anywhere you choose."
I find I made elaborate notes of all these arguments all that long time ago, merely for the
logical pleasure of disentangling an intellectual
injustice. I had no more idea of becoming a
Catholic than of becoming a cannibal. I imagined that I was merely pointing out that
justice should be done even to cannibals. I
imagined that I was noting certain fallacies
partly for the fun of the thing and partly for a
certain feeling of loyalty to the truth of things.
But as a matter of fact, looking back on these
notes (which I never published), it seems to
me that I took a tremendous amount of trouble about it if I really regarded it as a trifle;
and taking trouble has certainly never been a

particular weakness of mine. It seems to me that something was already working subconsciously to keep me more interested in fallacies about this particular topic than in fallacies about Free Trade or Female Suffrage or the House of Lords. Anyhow, that is the first stage in my own case and I think in many other cases: the stage of simply wishing to protect Papists from slander and oppression, not (consciously at least) because they hold any particular truth, but because they suffer from a particular accumulation of falsehood. The second stage is that in which the convert begins to be conscious not only of the falsehood but the truth, and is enormously excited to find that there is far more of it than he would ever have expected. This is not so much a stage as a progress; and it goes on pretty rapidly but often for a long time. It consists in discovering what a very large number of lively and interesting ideas there are in the Catholic philosophy, that a great many of them commend themselves at once to his sympathies, and that even those which he would not accept have something to be said for them justifying their acceptance. This process, which may be called

discovering the Catholic Church, is perhaps the
most pleasant and straightforward part of the
business; easier than joining the Catholic
Church and much easier than trying to live
the Catholic life. It is like discovering a new
continent full of strange flowers and fantastic
animals, which is at once wild and hospitable.
To give anything like a full account of that
process would simply be to discuss about half
a hundred Catholic ideas and institutions in
turn. I might remark that much of it consists
of the act of translation; of discovering the real
meaning of words, which the Church uses
rightly and the world uses wrongly. For instance,
the convert discovers that "scandal" does not
mean "gossip"; and the sin of causing it does
not mean that it is always wicked to set silly
old women wagging their tongues. Scandal
means scandal, what it originally meant in
Greek and Latin: the tripping up of somebody
else when he is trying to be good. Or he will
discover that phrases like "counsel of perfec-
tion" or "venial sin," which mean nothing at
all in the newspapers, mean something quite
intelligent and interesting in the manuals of
moral theology. He begins to realise that it is

the secular world that spoils the sense of words; and he catches an exciting glimpse of the real case for the iron immortality of the Latin Mass. It is not a question between a dead language and a living language, in the sense of an everlasting language. It is a question between a dead language and a dying language; an inevitably degenerating language. It is these numberless glimpses of great ideas, that have been hidden from the convert by the prejudices of his provincial culture, that constitute the adventurous and varied second stage of the conversion. It is, broadly speaking, the stage in which the man is unconsciously trying to be converted. And the third stage is perhaps the truest and the most terrible. It is that in which the man is trying not to be converted.

He has come too near to the truth, and has forgotten that truth is a magnet, with the powers of attraction and repulsion. He is filled with a sort of fear, which makes him feel like a fool who has been patronising "Popery" when he ought to have been awakening to the reality of Rome. He discovers a strange and alarming fact, which is perhaps implied in Newman's

interesting lecture on Blanco White[27] and the
two ways of attacking Catholicism. Anyhow,
it is a truth that Newman and every other convert has probably found in one form or another.
It is impossible to be just to the Catholic
Church. The moment men cease to pull against
it they feel a tug towards it. The moment they
cease to shout it down they begin to listen to
it with pleasure. The moment they try to be
fair to it they begin to be fond of it. But when
that affection has passed a certain point it begins
to take on the tragic and menacing grandeur
of a great love affair. The man has exactly the
same sense of having committed or compro-
mised himself; of having been in a sense
entrapped, even if he is glad to be entrapped.
But for a considerable time he is not so much
glad as simply terrified. It may be that this real
psychological experience has been misunder-
stood by stupider people and is responsible for
all that remains of the legend that Rome is a
mere trap. But that legend misses the whole
point of the psychology. It is not the Pope who

[27]Joseph Blanco White (1775–1841) was a Spanish-born priest
who abandoned Catholicism, settled in England and published *Evi-
dences Against Catholicism* in 1825.

has set the trap or the priests who have baited it. The whole point of the position is that the trap is simply the truth. The whole point is that the man himself has made his way towards the trap of truth, and not the trap that has run after the man. All steps except the last step he has taken eagerly on his own account, out of interest in the truth; and even the last step, or the last stage, only alarms him because it is so very true. If I may refer once more to a personal experience, I may say that I for one was never less troubled by doubts than in the last phase, when I was troubled by fears. Before that final delay I had been detached and ready to regard all sorts of doctrines with an open mind. Since that delay has ended in decision, I have had all sorts of changes in mere mood; and I think I sympathise with doubts and difficulties more than I did before. But I had no doubts or difficulties just before. I had only fears; fears of something that had the finality and simplicity of suicide. But the more I thrust the thing into the back of my mind, the more certain I grew of what Thing it was. And by a paradox that does not frighten me now in the least, it may be that I shall never again have such absolute assurance that the thing is true as I had when I made my last effort to deny it.

There is a postscript or smaller point to be added here to this paradox; which I know that many will misunderstand. Becoming a Catholic broadens the mind. It especially broadens the mind about the reasons for becoming a Catholic. Standing in the centre where all roads meet, a man can look down each of the roads in turn and realise that they come from all points of the heavens. As long as he is still marching along his own road, that is the only road that can be seen, or sometimes even imagined. For instance, many a man who is not yet a Catholic calls himself a Mediævalist. But a man who is only a Mediævalist is very much broadened by becoming a Catholic. I am myself a Mediævalist, in the sense that I think modern life has a great deal to learn from mediæval life; that Guilds are a better social system than Capitalism; that friars are far less offensive than philanthropists. But I am a much more reasonable and moderate Mediævalist than I was when I was only a Mediævalist. For instance, I felt it necessary to be perpetually pitting Gothic architecture against Greek architecture, because it was necessary to back up Christians against Pagans. But now I am in no such fuss and I know what Coventry Patmore[28] meant when he said calmly that it would have been quite as Catholic to decorate his mantelpiece with the Venus of Milo as with the Virgin. As a Mediævalist I am still proudest of the Gothic; but as a Catholic I am proud of the Baroque. That intensity which seems almost narrow because it comes to the point, like a mediæval window, is very representative of that last concentration that comes just before conversion. At the last moment of all, the convert often feels as if he were looking through a leper's window. He is looking through a little crack or crooked hole that seems to grow smaller as he stares at it; but it is an opening that looks towards the Altar. Only, when he has entered the Church, he finds that the Church is much larger inside than it is outside. He has left behind him the lop-sidedness of lepers' windows and even in a sense the narrowness of Gothic doors; and he is under vast domes as open as the Renaissance and as universal as the

---

[28] Coventry Patmore (1823–1896) was an English poet and convert to Catholicism.

Republic of the world. He can say in a sense unknown to all modern men certain ancient and serene words: *Romanus civis sum;*[29] I am not a slave.

The point for the moment, however, is that there is generally an interval of intense nervousness, to say the least of it, before this normal heritage is reached. To a certain extent it is a fear which attaches to all sharp and irrevocable decisions; it is suggested in all the old jokes about the shakiness of the bridegroom at the wedding or the recruit who takes the shilling and gets drunk partly to celebrate, but partly also to forget it. But it is the fear of a fuller sacrament and a mightier army. He has, by the nature of the case, left a long way behind him the mere clumsy idea that the sacrament will poison him or the army will kill him. He has probably passed the point, though he does generally pass it at some time, when he wonders whether the whole business is an extraordinarily intelligent and ingenious confidence trick. He is not now in the condition which may be called the last phase of real doubt. I

---

[29] *Romanus civis sum* is Latin for "I am a citizen of Rome."

mean that in which he wondered whether the thing that everybody told him was too bad to be tolerable, is not too good to be true. Here again the recurrent principle is present; and the obstacle is the very opposite of that which Protestant propaganda has pointed out. If he still has the notion of being trapped, he has no longer any notion of being tricked. He is not afraid of finding the Church out, but rather of the Church finding him out.

This note on the stages of conversion is necessarily very negative and inadequate. There is in the last second of time or hair's breadth of space, before the iron leaps to the magnet, an abyss full of all the unfathomable forces of the universe. The space between doing and not doing such a thing is so tiny and so vast. It is only possible here to give the reasons for Catholicism, not the cause of Catholicism. I have tried to suggest here some of the enlightenments and experiences which gradually teach those who have been taught to think ill of the Church to begin to think well of her. That anything described as so bad should turn out to be so good is itself a rather arresting process having a savour of something sensational and strange. To come to curse and remain to bless, to come to scoff and remain to pray, is always welcome in a spirit of wonder and the glow of an unexpected good.

But it is one thing to conclude that Catholicism is good and another to conclude that it is right. It is one thing to conclude that it is right and another to conclude that it is always right. I had never believed the tradition that it was diabolical; I had soon come to doubt the idea that it was inhuman, but that would only have left me with the obvious inference that it was human. It is a considerable step from that to the inference that it is divine. When we come to that conviction of divine authority, we come to the more mysterious matter of divine aid. In other words, we come to the unfathomable idea of grace and the gift of faith; and I have not the smallest intention of attempting to fathom it. It is a theological question of the utmost complexity; and it is one thing to feel it as a fact and another to define it as a truth. One or two points about the preliminary dispositions that prepare the mind for it are all that need be indicated here. To begin with, there is one sense in which the blackest bigots are really the best philosophers. The Church really is like Antichrist in the sense that it is as unique as Christ. Indeed, if it be not Christ it probably is Antichrist; but certainly it is not Moses or Mahomet or Buddha or Plato or Pythagoras. The more we see of humanity, the more we sympathise with humanity, the more we shall see that when it is simply human it is simply heathen; and the names of its particular local gods or tribal prophets or highly respectable sages are a secondary matter compared with that human and heathen character. In the old paganism of Europe, in the existing paganism of Asia, there have been gods and priests and prophets and sages of all sorts; but not another institution of this sort. The pagan cults die very slowly; they do not return very rapidly. They do not make the sort of claim that is made at a crisis; and then make the same claim again and again at crisis after crisis throughout the whole history of the earth. All that people fear in the Church, all that they hate in her, all against which they most harden their hearts and sometimes (one is tempted to say) thicken their heads, all that has made people consciously and unconsciously treat the Catholic Church as a *peril*, is the evidence that there is something here that we cannot look on at languidly and with detachment, as we might look on at Hottentots dancing at the new moon or Chinamen burning paper in porcelain temples. The Chinaman and the tourist can be on the best of terms on a basis of mutual scorn. But in the duel of the Church and the world is no such shield of contempt. The Church will not consent to scorn the soul of a coolie or even a tourist; and the measure of the madness with which men hate her is but their vain attempt to despise.

Another element, far more deep and delicate and hard to describe, is the immediate connection of what is most awful and archaic with what is most intimate and individual. It is a miracle in itself that anything so huge and historic in date and design should be so fresh in the affections. It is as if a man found his own parlour and fireside in the heart of the Great Pyramid. It is as if a child's favourite doll turned out to be the oldest sacred image in the world, worshipped in Chaldea or Nineveh. It is as if a girl to whom a man made love in a garden were also, in some dark and double fashion, a

statue standing for ever in a square. It is just
here that all those things which were regarded
as weakness come in as the fulness of strength.
Everything that men called sentimental in
Roman Catholic religion, its keepsakes, its small
flowers and almost tawdry trinkets, its figures
with merciful gestures and gentle eyes, its avow-
edly popular pathos and all that Matthew
Arnold meant by Christianity with its "reliev-
ing tears"—all this is a sign of sensitive and
vivid vitality in anything so vast and settled
and systematic. There is nothing quite like this
warmth, as in the warmth of Christmas, amid
ancient hills hoary with such snows of antiquity. It can address even God Almighty with
diminutives. In all its varied vestments it wears
its Sacred Heart upon its sleeve. But to those
who know that it is full of these lively affections, like little leaping flames, there is something of almost ironic satisfaction in the stark
and primitive size of the thing, like some pre-
historic monster; in its spires and mitres like
the horns of giant herds or its colossal corner-
stones like the four feet of an elephant. It would
be easy to write a merely artistic study of the
strange externals of the Roman religion, which

should make it seem as uncouth and unearthly
as Aztec or African religion. It would be easy
to talk of it as if it were really some sort of
mammoth or monster elephant, older than the
Ice Age, towering over the Stone Age; his very
lines traced, it would seem, in the earthquakes
or landslides of some older creation, his very
organs and outer texture akin to unrecorded
patterns of vegetation and air and light—the
last residuum of a lost world. But the prehis-
toric monster is in the Zoölogical Gardens and
not in the Natural History Museum. The
extinct animal is still alive. And anything out-
landish and unfamiliar in its form accentuates
the startling naturalness and familiarity of its
mind, as if the Sphinx began suddenly to talk
of the topics of the hour. The super-elephant
is not only a tame animal but a pet; and a young
child shall lead him.

This antithesis between all that is formida-
ble and remote and all that is personally rele-
vant and realistically tender is another of those
converging impressions which meet in the
moment of conviction. But of all these things,
that come nearest to the actual transition of
the gift of faith, it is far harder to write than

of the rationalistic and historical preliminaries of the enquiry. It is only with those preliminary dispositions towards the truth that I claim to deal here. In the chapters that follow I propose to touch upon two of the larger considerations of this class, not because they are in themselves any larger than many other immense aspects of so mighty a theme, but because they happen to balance each other and form a sort of antithesis very typical of all Catholic truth. In the first of the two chapters I shall try to point out how it is that when we praise the Church for her greatness we do not merely mean her largeness but, in a rather notable and unique sense, her universality. We mean her power of being cosmos and containing other things. And in the second chapter I shall point out what may seem to disturb this truth but really balances it. I mean the fact that we value the Church because she is a Church Militant; and sometimes even because she militates against ourselves. She is something more than the cosmos, in the sense of completed nature or completed human nature. She proves that she is something more by sometimes being right where they are wrong. These two aspects must be considered separately, though they come together to form the full conviction that comes just before conversion. But in this chapter I have merely noted down a few points or stages of the conversion considered as a practical process; and especially those three stages of it through which many a Protestant or Agnostic must have passed. Many a man, looking back cheerfully on them now, will not be annoyed if I call the first, patronising the Church; and the second, discovering the Church; and the third, running away from the Church. When those three phases are over, a larger truth begins to come into sight; it is much too large to describe and we will proceed to describe it.

IV

THE WORLD INSIDE OUT

The first fallacy about the Catholic Church is the idea that it is a church. I mean that it is a church in the sense in which the Nonconformist newspapers talk about The Churches. I do not intend any expression of contempt about The Churches; nor is it an expression of contempt to say that it would be more convenient to call them the sects. This is true in a much deeper and more sympathetic sense than may at first appear; but to begin with, it is certainly true in a perfectly plain and historical sense, which has nothing to do with sympathy at all. Thus, for instance, I have much more sympathy for small nationalities than I have for small sects. But it is simply a historical fact that the Roman Empire was the Empire and that it was not a small nationality. And it is simply a historical fact that the Roman Church is the

Church and is not a sect. Nor is there anything narrow or unreasonable in saying that the Church is the Church. It may be a good thing that the Roman Empire broke up into nations; but it certainly was not one of the nations into which it broke up. And even a person who thinks it fortunate that the Church broke up into sects ought to be able to distinguish between the little things he likes and the big thing he has broken. As a matter of fact, in the case of things so large, so unique and so creative of the culture about them as were the Roman Empire and the Roman Church, it is not controversial but simply correct to confine the one word to the one example. Everybody who originally used the word "Empire" used it of that Empire; everybody who used the word "Ecclesia" used it of that Ecclesia. There may have been similar things in other places, but they could not be called by the same name for the simple reason that they were not named in the same language. We know what we mean by a Roman Emperor; we can if we like talk of a Chinese Emperor, just as we can if we like take a particular sort of a Mandarin and say he is equivalent to a Marquis. But we

never can be certain that he is exactly equivalent; for the thing we are thinking about is
peculiar to our own history and in that sense
stands alone. Now in that, if in no other sense,
the Catholic Church stands alone. It does not
merely belong to a class of Christian churches.
It does not merely belong to a class of human
religions. Considered quite coldly and impar-
tially, as by a man from the moon, it is much
more *sui generis* than that. It is, if the critic
chooses to think so, the ruin of an attempt at
a Universal Religion which was bound to fail.
But calling the wreckers to break up a ship
does not turn the ship into one of its own
timbers; and cutting Poland up into three pieces
does not make Poland the same as Posen.

But in a much more profound and philosophical sense this notion that the Church is
one of the sects is the great fallacy of the whole
affair. It is a matter more psychological and
more difficult to describe. But it is perhaps the
most sensational of the silent upheavals or rever-
sals in the mind that constitute the revolution
called conversion. Every man conceives himself as moving about in a cosmos of some kind;
and the man of the days of my youth walked

about in a kind of vast and airy Crystal Palace[30] in which there were exhibits set side by side. The cosmos, being made of glass and iron, was partly transparent and partly colourless; anyhow, there was something negative about it; arching over all our heads, a roof as remote as a sky, it seemed to be impartial and impersonal. Our attention was fixed on the exhibits, which were all carefully ticketed and arranged in rows; for it was the age of science. Here stood all the religions in a row—the churches or sects or whatever we called them; and towards the end of the row there was a particularly dingy and dismal one, with a pointed roof half fallen in and pointed windows most broken with stones by passers-by; and we were told that this particular exhibit was the Roman Catholic Church. Some of us were sorry for it and even fancied it had been rather badly used; most of us regarded it as dirty and disreputable; a few of us even pointed out that many details in the ruin were artistically beautiful or architecturally important. But most people

[30]The Crystal Palace was a vast building erected in London in 1851 to house the first international exhibition of the products and machines of the industrial age.

preferred to deal at other and more business-like booths; at the Quaker shop of Peace and Plenty or the Salvation Army store where the showman beats the big drum outside. Now conversion consists very largely, on its intellectual side, in the discovery that all that picture of equal creeds inside an indifferent cosmos is quite false. It is not a question of comparing the merits and defects of the Quaker meeting-house set beside the Catholic cathedral. It is the Quaker meeting-house that is inside the Catholic cathedral; it is the Catholic cathedral that covers everything like the vault of the Crystal Palace; and it is when we look up at the vast distant dome covering all the exhibits that we trace the Gothic roof and the pointed windows. In other words, Quakerism is but a temporary form of Quietism[31] which has arisen technically outside the Church as the Quietism of Fenelon appeared technically inside the Church. But both were in themselves temporary and would have, like Fenelon, sooner or later to return to the Church in order to live.

[31] Quietism was a seventeenth-century form of mystical contemplation. François Fénelon (1651–1715), archbishop of Cambrai, championed it in France.

The principle of life in all these variations of
Protestantism, in so far as it is not a principle
of death, consists of what remained in them
of Catholic Christendom; and to Catholic
Christendom they have always returned to be
recharged with vitality. I know that this will
sound like a statement to be challenged; but it
is true. The return of Catholic ideas to the
separated parts of Christendom was often indeed indirect. But though the influence came
through many centres, it always came from
one. It came through the Romantic Movement, a glimpse of the mere picturesqueness
of mediævalism; but it is something more than
an accident that Romances, like Romance lan-
guages, are named after Rome. Or it came
through the instinctive reaction of old-fashioned
people like Johnson or Scott or Cobbett,[32]
wishing to save old elements that had originally been Catholic against a progress that was
merely Capitalist. But it led them to denounce
that Capitalist progress and become, like Cobbett, practical foes of Protestantism without

[32] William Cobbett (1763–1835) was an English political radical
and agricultural reformer, whose best-known book was *Rural Rides*
(1830).

being practising followers of Catholicism. Or it came from the Pre-Raphaelites[33] or the opening of continental art and culture by Matthew Arnold and Morris[34] and Ruskin and the rest. But examine the actual make-up of the mind of a good Quaker or Congregational minister at this moment, and compare it with the mind of such a dissenter in the Little Bethel before such culture came. And you will see how much of his health and happiness he owes to Ruskin and what Ruskin owed to Giotto; to Morris and what Morris owed to Chaucer; to fine scholars of his own school like Philip Wicksteed, and what they owe to Dante and St. Thomas. Such a man will still sometimes talk of the Middle Ages as the Dark Ages. But the Dark Ages have improved the wallpaper on his wall and the dress on his wife and all the whole dingy and vulgar life which

[33] The Pre-Raphaelite Brotherhood, a movement to infuse art with morality, flourished in mid-nineteenth-century England. Its members, most prominent of whom were William Holman Hunt, John Everett Millais and Dante Gabriel Rossetti, contended that the degeneration of Western art had begun in the Renaissance with Raphael.

[34] William Morris (1834–1896) was an English poet, novelist, artist and prominent advocate of socialism.

he lived in the days of Stiggins[35] and Brother Tadger. For he also is a Christian and lives only by the life of Christendom.

It is not easy to express this enormous inversion which I have here tried to suggest in the image of a world turned inside out. I mean that the thing which had been stared at as a small something swells out and swallows everything. Christendom is in the literal sense a continent. We come to feel that it contains everything, even the things in revolt against itself. But it is perhaps the most towering intellectual transformation of all and the one that it is hardest to undo even for the sake of argument. It is almost impossible even in imagination to reverse that reversal. Another way of putting it is to say that we have come to regard all these historical figures as characters in Catholic history, even if they are not Catholics. And in a certain sense, the historical as distinct from the theological sense, they never do cease to be Catholic. They are not people who have really created something entirely new, until they actually pass the border of reason and create

[35] Stiggins was a character in Dickens' *The Pickwick Papers*.

more or less crazy nightmares. But nightmares do not last; and most of them even now are in various stages of waking up. Protestants are Catholics gone wrong; that is what is really meant by saying they are Christians. Sometimes they have gone very wrong; but not often have they gone right ahead with their own particular wrong. Thus a Calvinist is a Catholic obsessed with the Catholic idea of the sovereignty of God. But when he makes it mean that God wishes particular people to be damned, we may say with all restraint that he has become a rather morbid Catholic. In point of fact he is a diseased Catholic; and the disease left to itself would be death or madness. But, as a matter of fact, the disease did not last long, and is itself now practically dead. But every step he takes back towards humanity is a step back towards Catholicism. Thus a Quaker is a Catholic obsessed with the Catholic idea of gentle simplicity and truth. But when he made it mean that it is a lie to say "you" and an act of idolatry to take off your hat to a lady, it is not too much to say that whether or not he had a hat off, he certainly had a tile loose. But as a matter of fact he himself found it necessary to dispense with the eccentricity (and the hat) and to leave the straight road that would have led him to a lunatic asylum. Only every step he takes back towards common sense is a step back towards Catholicism. In so far as he was right he was a Catholic; and in so far as he was wrong he has not himself been able to remain a Protestant.

To us, therefore, it is henceforth impossible to think of the Quaker as a figure at the beginning of a new Quaker history or the Calvinist as the founder of a new Calvinistic world. It is quite obvious to us that they are simply characters in our own Catholic history, only characters who caused a great deal of trouble by trying to do something that we could do better and that they did not really do at all. Now some may suppose that this can be maintained of the older sects like Calvinists and Quakers, but cannot be maintained of modern movements like those of Socialists or Spiritualists. But they will be quite wrong. The covering or continental character of the Church applies just as much to modern manias as to the old religious manias; it applies quite as much to Materialists or Spiritualists as to Puritans. In

all of them you find that some Catholic dogma
is, first, taken for granted; then exaggerated into
an error; and then generally reacted against and
rejected as an error, bringing the individual
in question a few steps back again on the
homeward road. And this is almost always the
mark of such a heretic; that while he will wildly
question any other Catholic dogma, he never
dreams of questioning his own favourite Catholic dogma and does not even seem to know
that it could be questioned. It never occurred
to the Calvinist that anybody might use his
liberty to deny or limit the divine omnipotence, or to the Quaker that anyone could question the supremacy of simplicity. That is exactly
the situation of the Socialist. Bolshevism and
every shade of any such theory of brotherhood is based upon one unfathomably mystical Catholic dogma; the equality of men. The
Communists stake everything on the equality
of man, as the Calvinists staked everything on
the omnipotence of God. They ride it to death
as the others rode their dogma to death, turn-
ing their horse into a nightmare. But it never
seems to occur to them that some people do
not believe in the Catholic dogma of the

mystical equality of men. Yet there are many, even among Christians, who are so heretical as to question it. The Socialists get into a great tangle when they try to apply it; they compromise with their own ideals; they modify their own doctrine; and so find themselves, like the Quakers and the Calvinists, after all their extreme extravagances, a day's march nearer Rome.

In short, the story of these sects is not one of straight lines striking outwards and onwards, though if it were they would all be striking in different directions. It is a pattern of curves continually returning into the continent and common life of their and our civilisation; and the summary of that civilisation and central sanity is the philosophy of the Catholic Church. To us, Spiritualists are men studying the existence of spirits, in a brief and blinding oblivion of the existence of evil spirits. They are, as it were, people just educated enough to have heard of ghosts but not educated enough to have heard of witches. If the evil spirits succeed in stopping their education and stunting their minds, they may of course go on for ever repeating silly messages from Plato and doggerel verses from Milton. But if they do go a step or two further, instead of marking time on the borderland, their next step will be to learn what the Church could have taught. To us, Christian Scientists are simply people with one idea, which they have never learnt to balance and combine with all the other ideas. That is why the wealthy business man so often becomes a Christian Scientist. He is not used to ideas and one idea goes to his head, like one glass of wine to a starving man. But the Catholic Church is used to living with ideas and walks among all those very dangerous wild beasts with the poise and the lifted head of a lion-tamer. The Christian Scientist can go on monotonously repeating his one idea and remain a Christian Scientist. But if ever he really goes on to any other ideas, he will be so much the nearer to being a Catholic.

When the convert has once seen the world like that, with one balance of ideas and a number of other ideas that have left it and lost their balance, he does not in fact experience any of the inconveniences that he might reasonably have feared before that silent but stunning revolution. He is not worried by being told that there is something in Spiritualism or something

in Christian Science. He knows there is something in everything. But he is moved by the
more impressive fact that he finds everything
in something. And he is quite sure that if these
investigators really are looking for everything,
and not merely looking for anything, they will
be more and more likely to look for it in the
same place. In that sense he is far less worried
about them than he was when he thought that
one or other of them might be the only person having any sort of communication with
the higher mysteries and obviously rather capable of making a mess of it. He is no more likely
to be overawed by the fact that Mrs. Eddy[36]
achieved spiritual healing or Mr. Home[37]
achieved bodily levitation than a fully dressed
gentleman in Bond Street would be overawed
by the top-hat on the head of a naked savage.
A top-hat may be a good hat but it is a bad
costume. And a magnetic trick may be a suf-
ficient sensation but it is a very insufficient philosophy. He is no more envious of a Bolshevist
for making a revolution than of a beaver for

[36] Mary Baker Eddy (1821–1910) was the American founder of
Christian Science.

[37] Daniel Home (1833–1886) was a noted English Spiritualist.

making a dam; for he knows his own civilisation can make things on a pattern not quite so simple or so monotonous. But he believes this of his civilisation and his religion and not merely of himself. There is nothing supercilious about his attitude; because he is well aware that he has only scratched the surface of the spiritual estate that is now open to him. In other words, the convert does not in the least abandon investigation or even adventure. He does not think he knows everything, nor has he lost curiosity about the things he does not know. But experience has taught him that he will find nearly everything somewhere inside that estate and that a very large number of people are finding next to nothing outside it. For the estate is not only a formal garden or an ordered farm; there is plenty of hunting and fishing on it, and, as the phrase goes, very good sport.

For this is one of the very queerest of the common delusions about what happens to the convert. In some muddled way people have confused the natural remarks of converts, about having found moral peace, with some idea of their having found mental rest, in the sense of mental inaction. They might as well say that a man who has completely recovered his health, after an attack of palsy or St. Vitus' dance, signalises his healthy state by sitting absolutely still like a stone. Recovering his health means recovering his power of moving in the right way as distinct from the wrong way; but he will probably move a great deal more than before. To become a Catholic is not to leave off thinking, but to learn how to think. It is so in exactly the same sense in which to recover from palsy is not to leave off moving but to learn how to move. The Catholic convert has for the first time a starting-point for straight and strenuous thinking. He has for the first time a way of testing the truth in any question that he raises. As the world goes, especially at present, it is the other people, the heathen and the heretics, who seem to have every virtue except the power of connected thought. There was indeed a brief period when a small minority did some hard thinking on the heathen or heretical side. It barely lasted from the time of Voltaire to the time of Huxley. It has now entirely disappeared. What is now called free thought is valued, not because it is free thought, but because it is freedom from thought; because it is free thoughtlessness.

Nothing is more amusing to the convert, when his conversion has been complete for some time, than to hear the speculations about when or whether he will repent of the conversion; when he will be sick of it, how long he will stand it, at what stage of his external exasperation he will start up and say he can bear it no more. For all this is founded on that optical illusion about the outside and the inside which I have tried to sketch in this chapter. The outsiders, stand by and see, or think they see, the convert entering with bowed head a sort of small temple which they are convinced is fitted up inside like a prison, if not a torture-chamber. But all they really know about it is that he has passed through a door. They do not know that he has not gone into the inner darkness, but out into the broad daylight. It is he who is, in the beautiful and beatific sense of the word, an outsider. He does not want to go into a larger room, because he does not know of any larger room to go into. He knows of a large number of much smaller rooms, each of which is labelled as being very large; but he is quite sure he would be cramped in any of them. Each of them professes to be a complete cosmos or scheme of all things; but then so does the cosmos of the Clapham Sect[38] or the Clapton Agapemone.[39] Each of them is supposed to be domed with the sky or painted inside with all the stars. But each of these cosmic systems or machines seems to him much smaller and even much simpler than the broad and balanced universe in which he lives. One of them is labelled Agnostic; but he knows by experience that it has not really even the freedom of ignorance. It is a wheel that must always go round without a single jolt of miraculous interruption—a circle that must not be squared by any higher mathematics of mysticism; a machine that must be scoured as clean of all spirits as if it were the avowed machine of materialism. In living in a world with two orders, the supernatural and the natural, the convert feels he is living in a larger world and does not feel any temptation to crawl back into a

[38] The Clapham Sect was a group of English reformers who crusaded against various social evils, especially the international slave trade. The group, which originated in the 1790s, took its name from its meeting place, Henry Thornton's house in Clapham Common. Its most significant member was William Wilberforce (1759–1833).

[39] The Clapton Agapemone was a nineteenth-century English communal sect headed by Henry Prince.

smaller one. One of them is labelled Theosophi-
cal or Buddhistic; but he knows by experience that it is only the same sort of wearisome
wheel used for spiritual things instead of mate-
rial things. Living in a world where he is free
to do anything, even to go to the devil, he
does not see why he should tie himself to the
wheel of a mere destiny. One of them is labelled
Humanitarian; but he knows that such human-
itarians have really far less experience of humanity. He knows that they are thinking almost
entirely of men as they are at this moment
in modern cities, and have nothing like the
huge human interest of what began by being
preached to legionaries in Palestine and is still
being preached to peasants in China. So clear
is this perception that I have sometimes put it
to myself, as something between a melancholy
meditation and a joke. "Where *should* I go now,
if I did leave the Catholic Church?" I certainly would not go to any of those little social
sects which only express one idea at a time,
because that idea happens to be fashionable at
the moment. The best I could hope for would
be to wander away into the woods and become,
not a Pantheist (for that is also a limitation and

a bore) but rather a pagan, in the mood to cry out that some particular mountain peak or flowering fruit tree was sacred and a thing to be worshipped. That at least would be beginning all over again; but it would bring me back to the same problem in the end. If it was reasonable to have a sacred tree it was not unreasonable to have a sacred crucifix; and if the god was to be found on one peak he may as reasonably be found under one spire. To find a new religion is sooner or later to have found one; and why should I have been discontented with the one I had found? Especially, as I said in the first words of this essay, when it is the one old religion which seems capable of remaining new.

I know very well that if I went upon that journey I should either despair or return; and that none of the trees would ever be a substitute for the real sacred tree. Paganism is better than pantheism, for paganism is free to imagine divinities, while pantheism is forced to pretend, in a priggish way, that all things are equally divine. But I should not imagine any divinity that was sufficiently divine. I seem to know that weary return through the woodlands; for

I think in some symbolic fashion I have walked that road before. For as I have tried to confess here without excessive egotism, I think I am the sort of man who came to Christ from Pan and Dionysus and not from Luther or Laud;[40] that the conversion I understand is that of the pagan and not the Puritan; and upon that antique conversion is founded the whole world that we know. It is a transformation far more vast and tremendous than anything that has been meant for many years past, at least in England and America, by a sectarian controversy or a doctrinal division. On the height of that ancient empire and that international experience, humanity had a vision. It has not had another; but only quarrels about that one. Paganism was the largest thing in the world and Christianity was larger; and everything else has been comparatively small.

---

[40] William Laud (1573–1645), archbishop of Canterbury and persecutor of the Puritans, was executed for his support of King Charles I.

V

THE EXCEPTION PROVES THE RULE

The Catholic Church is the only thing which saves a man from the degrading slavery of being a child of his age. I have compared it with the New Religions; but this is exactly where it differs from the New Religions. The New Religions are in many ways suited to the new conditions; but they are only suited to the new conditions. When those conditions shall have changed in only a century or so, the points upon which alone they insist at present will have become almost pointless. If the Faith has all the freshness of a new religion, it has all the richness of an old religion; it has especially all the reserves of an old religion. So far as that is concerned, its antiquity is alone a great advantage, and especially a great advantage for purposes of renovation and youth. It is only by the analogy of animal bodies that we suppose that old things must be stiff. It is a mere metaphor from bones and arteries. In an intellectual sense old things are flexible. Above all, they are various and have many alternatives to offer. There is a sort of rotation of crops in religious history; and old fields can lie fallow for a while and then be worked again. But when the new religion or any such notion has sown its one crop of wild oats, which the wind generally blows away, it is barren. A thing as old as the Catholic Church has an accumulated armoury and treasury to choose from; it can pick and choose among the centuries and brings one age to the rescue of another. It can call in the old world to redress the balance of the new.

Anyhow, the New Religions are suited to the new world; and this is their most damning defect. Each religion is produced by contemporary causes than can be clearly pointed out. Socialism is a reaction against Capitalism. Spiritualism is a reaction against Materialism; it is also in its intensified form merely the trail of the tragedy of the Great War. But there is a somewhat more subtle sense in which the very fitness of the new creeds makes them unfit; their very acceptability makes them inacceptable. Thus they all profess to be progressive because the peculiar boast of their peculiar period was progress; they claim to be democratic because our political system still rather pathetically claims to be democratic. They rushed to a reconciliation with science, which was often only a premature surrender to science. They hastily divested themselves of anything considered dowdy or old-fashioned in the way of vesture or symbol. They claimed to have bright services and cheery sermons; the churches competed with the cinemas; the churches even became cinemas. In its more moderate form the mood was merely one of praising natural pleasures, such as the enjoyment of nature and even the enjoyment of human nature. These are excellent things and this is an excellent liberty; and yet it has its limitations.

We do not really want a religion that is right where we are right. What we want is a religion that is right where we are wrong. In these current fashions it is not really a question of the religion allowing us liberty; but (at the best) of the liberty allowing us a religion. These people merely take the modern mood, with much in it that is amiable and much that is anarchical and much that is merely dull and obvious, and then require any creed to be cut down to fit that mood. But the mood would exist even without the creed. They say they want a religion to be social, when they would be social without any religion. They say they want a religion to be practical, when they would be practical without any religion. They say they want a religion acceptable to science, when they would accept the science even if they did not accept the religion. They say they want a religion like this because they are like this already. They say they want it, when they mean that they could do without it.

It is a very different matter when a religion, in the real sense of a binding thing, binds men to their morality when it is not identical with their mood. It is very different when some of the saints preached social reconciliation to fierce and raging factions who could hardly bear the sight of each others' faces. It was a very different thing when charity was preached to pagans who really did not believe in it; just as it is a very different thing now, when chastity is preached to new pagans who do not believe in it. It is in those cases that we get the real grapple of religion; and it is in those cases that we get the peculiar and solitary triumph of the Catholic faith. It is not in merely being right when we are right, as in being cheerful or hopeful or humane. It is in having been right when we were wrong, and in the fact coming back upon us afterwards like a boomerang. One word that tells us what we do not know outweighs a thousand words that tell us what we do know. And the thing is all the more striking if we not only did not know it but could not believe it. It may seem a paradox to say that the truth teaches us more by the words we reject than by the words we receive. Yet the paradox is a parable of the simplest sort and familiar to us all; any example might be given of it. If a man tells us to avoid public houses, we think him a tiresome though perhaps a well-intentioned old party. If he tells us to use public houses, we recognise that he has a higher morality and presents an ideal that is indeed lofty, but perhaps a little too simple and obvious to need defence. But if a man tells us to avoid the one particular public house called The Pig and Whistle, on the left hand as you turn round by the pond, the direction may seem very dogmatic and arbitrary and showing insufficient process of argument. But if we then fling ourselves into The Pig and Whistle and are immediately poisoned with the gin or smothered in the feather-bed and robbed of our money, we recognise that the man who advised us did know something about it and had a cultivated and scientific knowledge of the public houses of the district. We think it even more, as we emerge half-murdered from The Pig and Whistle, if we originally rejected his warning as a silly superstition. The warning itself is almost more impressive if it was not justified by reasons, but only by results. There is something very notable about a thing which is arbitrary when it is also accurate. We may very easily forget, even while we fulfil, the advice that we thought was self-evident sense. But nothing can measure our mystical and unfathomable reverence for the advice that we thought was nonsense.

As will be seen in a moment, I do not mean in the least that the Catholic Church is arbitrary in the sense of never giving reasons; but I do mean that the convert is profoundly affected by the fact that, even when he did not see the reason, he lived to see that it was reasonable. But there is something even more singular than this, which it will be well to note as a part of the convert's experience. In many cases, as a matter of fact, he did originally have a glimpse of the reasons, even if he did not reason about them; but they were forgotten in the interlude when reason was clouded by rationalism. The point is not very easy to explain, and I shall be obliged to take merely personal examples in order to explain it. I mean that we have often had a premonition as well as a warning; and the fact often comes back to us after we have disregarded both. It is worth noting in connection with conversion, because the convert is often obstructed by a catchword which says that the Church crushes the conscience. The Church does not crush any man's conscience. It is the man who crushes his conscience and then finds out that it was right, when he has almost forgotten that he had one.

I will take two examples out of the new movements: Socialism and Spiritualism. Now it is perfectly true that when I first began to think seriously about Socialism, I was a Socialist. But it is equally true, and more important than it sounds, that before I had ever heard of

Socialism I was a strong anti-Socialist. I was what
has since been called a Distributist, though I did
not know it. When I was a child and dreamed
the usual dreams about kings and clowns and
robbers and policemen, I always conceived all
contentment and dignity as consisting in something compact and personal; in being king of the
castle or captain of the pirate ship or the man
who owned the shop or the robber who was safe
in the cavern. As I passed through boyhood I
always imagined battles for justice as being the
defence of special walls and houses and high
defiant shrines; and I embodied some of those
crude but coloured visions in a story called *The
Napoleon of Notting Hill*. All this happened, in
fancy at least, when I had never heard of Socialism and was a much better judge of it.

Shades of the prison-house began to close
and with them came a merely mechanical discussion as to how we were all to get out of
prison. *Then* indeed, in the darkness of the
dungeon, was heard the voice of Mr. Sid-
ney Webb,[41] telling us that we could only

[41]Sidney Webb (1859–1947) was one of the founders in 1884 of
the Fabian Society, an organization dedicated to establishing socialism in England through non-revolutionary, parliamentary means.

conceivably get out of our Capitalist captivity
with the patent Chubb key[42] of Collectivism.
Or to use a more exact metaphor, he told us
that we could only escape from our dark and
filthy cells of industrial slavery by melting all
our private latchkeys into one gigantic latchkey
as large as a battering ram. We did not really
like giving up our little private keys or local
attachments or love of our own possessions;
but we were quite convinced that social justice must be done somehow and could only
be done socialistically. I therefore became a
Socialist in the old days of the Fabian Society;
and so I think did everybody else worth talking about—except the Catholics. And the Catholics were an insignificant handful, the dregs
of a dead religion, essentially a superstition.
About this time appeared the Encyclical on
Labour by Leo XIII;[43] and nobody in our really
well-informed world took much notice of
it. Certainly the Pope spoke as strongly as
any Socialist could speak when he said that

[42] The Chubb key is used in a lock invented by an Englishman
named Chubb.

[43] Pope Leo XIII reigned from 1878 to 1903. His encyclical on
labour, *Rerum novarum* (1891), supported the rights of labor, called
for a just wage and defended trade unions.

Capitalism "laid on the toiling millions a yoke little better than slavery." But as the Pope was not a Socialist it was obvious that he had not read the right Socialist books and pamphlets; and we could not expect the poor old gentleman to know what every young man knew by this time—that Socialism was inevitable. That was a long time ago, and by a gradual process, mostly practical and political, which I have no intention of describing here, most of us began to realise that Socialism was not inevitable; that it was not really popular; that it was not the only way, or even the right way, of restoring the rights of the poor. We have come to the conclusion that the obvious cure for private property being given to the few is to see that it is given to the many; not to see that it is taken away from everybody or given in trust to the dear good politicians. Then, having discovered that fact as a fact, we look back at Leo XIII and discover in his old and dated document, of which we took no notice at the time, that he was saying then exactly what we are saying now. "As many as possible of the working classes should become owners." That is what I mean by the justification of arbitrary warning. If the Pope had said then exactly what we said and wanted him to say, we should not have really reverenced him then and we should have entirely repudiated him afterwards. He would only have marched with the million who accepted Fabianism; and with them he would have marched away. But when he saw a distinction we did not see then, and do see now, that distinction is decisive. It marks a disagreement more convincing than a hundred agreements. It is not that he was right when we were right, but that he was right when we were wrong.

The superficial critic of these things, noting that I am no longer a Socialist, will always say, "Of course, you are a Catholic and you are not allowed to be a Socialist." To which I answer emphatically, No. That is missing the whole point. The Church anticipated my experience; but it was experience and not only obedience. I am quite sure now from merely living in this world, and seeing something of Catholic peasants as well as Collectivist officials, that it is happier and healthier for most men to become owners than for them to give up all ownership to those officials. I do not follow the

State Socialist in his extreme belief in the State; but I have not ceased to be credulous about the State merely because I have become credulous about the Church. I believe less in the State because I know more of the statesmen. I cannot believe small property to be impossible after I have seen it. I cannot believe State management to be impeccable after I have seen it. It is not any authority, except what St. Thomas calls the authority of the senses, which tells me that the mere community of goods is a solution that is too much of a simplification. The Church has taught me, but I could not unteach myself; I have learned because I have lived, and I could not unlearn it. If I ceased to be a Catholic I could not again be a Communist.

As it happens, my story was almost exactly the same in connection with Spiritualism. There again I was modern when I was young, but not when I was very young. While I had a vague but innocent nursery religion still hanging about me, I regarded the first signs of these psychic and psychological things with mere repugnance. I hated the whole notion of mesmerism and magnetic tricks with the mind; I loathed their bulging eyes and stiff attitudes and

unnatural trances and the whole bag of tricks.
When I saw a girl I admired set down to crystal-
gazing, I was furious; I hardly knew why. Then
came the period when I wanted to know why,
when I examined my own reasons and found I
had none. I saw that it was inconsistent in science to revere research and forbid psychical
research. I saw that men of science were more
and more accepting these things and I went along
with my scientific age. I was never exactly a
Spiritualist, but I almost always defended Spiritualism. I experimented with a planchette, quite
enough to convince myself finally that some
things do happen that are not in the ordinary
sense natural. I have since come to think, for reasons that would require too much space to detail,
that it is not so much supernatural as unnatural
and even anti-natural. I believe the experiments
were bad for me; I believe they are bad for the
other experimentalists. But I found out the fact
long before I found out the Catholic Church or
the Catholic view of that question. Only, as I
have said, when I do find it out, I find it rather
impressive; for it is not the religion that was right
when I was right, but the religion that was right
when I was wrong.

But I wish to note about both those cases
that the common cant in the matter is emphatically not true. It is not true that the Church
crushed my natural conscience; it is not true
that the Church asked me to give up my individual ideal. It is not true that Collectivism
was ever my *ideal*. I do not believe it was ever
really anybody else's ideal. It was not an ideal
but a compromise; it was a concession to practical economists who told us that we could not
prevent poverty except by something uncom-
monly like slavery. State Socialism never came
natural to us; it never convinced us that it was
natural; it convinced us that it was necessary.
In exactly the same way Spiritualism never came
as something natural but only as something necessary. Each told us that it was *the only way*
into the promised land, in the one case of a
future life and the other of life in the future.
We did not like government departments and
tickets and registers; but we were told there
was no other way of reaching a better society. We did not like dark rooms and dubious
mediums and ladies tied up with rope, but we
were told there was no other way to reach a
better world. We were ready to crawl down a

municipal drain-pipe or through a spiritual sewer, because it was the only way to better things; the only way even to prove that there were better things. But the drain-pipe had never figured in our dreams like a tower of ivory or a house of gold, or even like the robbers' tower of our romantic boyhood or the solid and comfortable house of our matured experience. The Faith had not only been true all along, but it had been true to the first and the last things, to our unspoilt instincts and our conclusive experience; and it had condemned nothing but an interlude of intellectual snobbishness and surrender to the persuasions of pedantry. It had condemned nothing but what we ourselves should have come to condemn, though we might have condemned it too late.

The Church therefore never made my individual ideal impossible; it would be truer to say that she was the first to make it possible. The Encyclical's ideal had been much nearer my own instinct than the ideal I had consented to substitute for it. The Catholic suspicion of table-rapping was much more like my own original suspicion than it was like my own subsequent surrender. But in those two cases it is surely clear that the Catholic Church plays exactly the part that she professes to play: something that knows what we cannot be expected to know, but should probably accept if we really knew it. I am not in this case, any more than in the greater part of this study, referring to the things that are really best worth knowing. The supernatural truths are connected with the mystery of grace and are a matter for theologians; admittedly a rather delicate and difficult matter even for them. But though the transcendental truths are the most important they are not those that best illustrate this particular point, which concerns the decisions which can be more or less tested by experience. And of all those things that can be tested by experience I could tell the same story: that there was a time when I thought the Catholic doctrine was meaningless, but that even that was not the very earliest time, which was a time of greater simplicity, when I had a sort of glimpse of the meaning though I had never even heard of the doctrine. The world deceived me and the Church would at any time have undeceived me. The thing that a man may really shed at last like a superstition is the fashion of this world that passes away.

I could give many other examples, but I fear they would inevitably tend to be egotistical examples. Throughout this brief study I am under the double difficulty that all roads lead to Rome, but that each pilgrim is tempted to talk as if all roads had been like his own road. I could write a great deal, for instance, about my early wrestlings with the rather ridiculous dilemma which was put to me in my youth by the optimist and the pessimist. I promptly and properly refused to be a pessimist; and I therefore fell into the way of calling myself an optimist. Now I should not call myself either, and what is more important I can see that virtue may be entangled in both. But I think it is entangled; and I think that an older and simpler truth can loosen the tangle. But the point in the present connection is this; that before I had ever heard of optimists or pessimists I was something much more like what I am now than could be covered by either of those two pedantic words. In my childhood I assumed that cheerfulness was a good thing, but I also assumed that it was a bad thing not to protest against things that are really bad. After an interlude of intellectual formalism and false antithesis, I have come back to being able to think what I could then only feel. But I have realised that the protest can rise to a much more divine indignation and that the cheerfulness is but a faint suggestion of a much more divine joy. It is not so much that I have found I was wrong as that I have found out why I was right.

In this we find the supreme example of the exception that proves the rule. The rule, of which I have given a rough outline in the previous chapter, is that the Catholic philosophy is a universal philosophy found to fit anywhere with human nature and the nature of things. But even when it does not fit in with human nature it is found in the long run to favour something yet more fitting. It generally suits us, but where it does not suit us we learn to suit it, so long as we are alive enough to learn anything. In the rare cases where a reasonable man can really say that it cuts across his intelligence, it will generally be found that it is true, not only to truth, but even to his deepest instinct for truth. Education does not cease with conversion, but rather begins. The man does not cease to study because he has become convinced that certain things are worth studying; and these things include not only the orthodox values but even the orthodox vetoes. Strangely enough, in a sense, the forbidden fruit is often more fruitful than the free. It is more fruitful in the sense of a fascinating botanical study of why it is really poisonous. Thus, for the sake of an example, all healthy people have an instinct against usury; and the Church has only confirmed that instinct. But to learn how to define usury, to study what it is and to argue why it is wrong, is to have a liberal education, not only in political economy, but in the philosophy of Aristotle and the history of the Councils of Lateran.[44] There almost always is a human reason for all the merely human advice given by the Church to humanity; and to find out the principle of the thing is, among other things, one of the keenest of intellectual pleasures. But in any case the fact remains that the Church is right in the main in being tolerant in the main; but that where she is intolerant she is most right and even more reasonable. Adam lived in a garden where a

---

[44] The Councils of Lateran were five general councils of the Church, held at St. John Lateran church in Rome between 1123 and 1512.

thousand mercies were granted to him; but the
one inhibition was the greatest mercy of all.

In the same way, let the convert, or still more
the semi-convert, face any one fact that does
seem to him to deface the Catholic scheme as
a falsehood; and if he faces it long enough he
will probably find that it is the greatest truth
of all. I have found this myself in that extreme
logic of free will which is found in the fallen
angels and the possibility of perdition. Such
things are altogether beyond my imagination,
but the lines of logic go out towards them in
my reason. Indeed, I can undertake to justify
the whole Catholic theology, if I be granted
to start with the supreme sacredness and value
of two things: Reason and Liberty. It is an illuminating comment on current anti-Catholic
talk that they are the two things which most
people imagine to be forbidden to Catholics.

But the best way of putting what I mean is
to repeat what I have already said, in connection
with the satisfying scope of Catholic universality.
I cannot picture these theological ultimates and
I have not the authority or learning to define
them. But I still put the matter to myself thus:
Supposing I were so miserable as to lose the

Faith, could I go back to that cheap charity and crude optimism which says that every sin is a blunder, that evil cannot conquer or does not even exist? I could no more go back to those cushioned chapels than a man who has regained his sanity would willingly go back to a padded cell. I might cease to believe in a God of any kind; but I could not cease to think that a God who had made men and angels free was finer than one who coerced them into comfort. I might cease to believe in a future life of any kind; but I could not cease to think it was a finer doctrine that we choose and make our future life than that it is fitted out for us like an hotel and we are taken there in a celestial omnibus as compulsory as a Black Maria.[45] I know that Catholicism is too large for me, and I have not yet explored its beautiful or terrible truths. But I know that Universalism is too small for me; and I could not creep back into that dull safety, who have looked on the dizzy vision of liberty.

[45] The Black Maria was a van used in England to transport prisoners.

VI

A NOTE ON PRESENT PROSPECTS

On reconsidering these notes I find them to be far too personal; yet I do not know how any conception of conversion can be anything else. I do not profess to have any particular knowledge about the actual conditions and calculations of the Catholic movement at the moment. I do not believe that anybody else has any knowledge of what it will be like the next moment. Statistics are generally misleading and predictions are practically always false. But there is always a certain faint tradition of the thing called common sense; and so long as a glimmer of it remains, in spite of all journalism and State instruction, it is possible to appreciate what we call a reality. Nobody in his five wits will deny that at this moment conversion is a reality. Everybody knows that his

135

own social circle, which fifty years ago would have been a firm territory of Protestantism, perhaps hardening into rationalism or indifference but doing even that slowly and without conscious convulsion, has just lately shown a curious disposition to collapse softly and suddenly, first in one unexpected place and then in another, making great holes in that solid land and letting up the leaping flames of what was counted an extinct volcano. It is in everybody's experience, whether he is sad or glad or mad or merely indifferent, that these conversions seem to come of themselves in the most curious and apparently accidental quarters; Tom's wife, Harry's brother, Fanny's funny sister-in-law who went on the stage, Sam's eccentric uncle who studied military strategy—of each of these isolated souls we hear suddenly that it is isolated no longer. It is one with the souls militant and triumphant.

Against these things (which we know as facts and do not merely read as statistics) there is admittedly something to be set. It is what is commonly called leakage; and with a paragraph upon this point I will close these pages.

Father Ronald Knox,[46] with that felicity that is so good that the wit almost seems like good luck, has remarked that the Catholic Church really does have to get on by hook or crook. That is, by the hook of the fisherman and the crook of the shepherd; and it is the hook that has to catch the convert and the crook that has to keep him. He said in this connection that the conversions to the Church just now were so numerous that they would be obvious and overwhelming, like a landslide, if it were not that they were neutralised in mere numbers, or rather lessened in their full claim of numbers, by a certain amount of falling away in other directions. Now the first fact to realise is that it is in other directions, in totally different directions. Some people, especially young people, abandon practicing Catholicism. But none of them abandon it for Protestantism. All of them practically abandon it for paganism. Most of them abandon it for

---

[46]Monsignor Ronald Knox (1888–1957) was one of the most famous Anglican converts to Catholicism in twentieth-century England. He served as Catholic chaplain at Oxford University (1926–1939), produced a fresh translation of the Vulgate Bible, authored detective stories and became one of England's most articulate Catholic apologists.

something that is really rather too simple to be called an *ism* of any kind. They abandon it for things and not theories; and when they do have theories they may sometimes be Bolshevist theories or Futurist[47] theories, but they are practically never the theological theories of Protestantism. I will not say they leave Catholicism for beer and skittles; for Catholicism has never discouraged those Christian institutions as Protestantism sometimes has. They leave it to have a high old time; and considering what a muddle we have made of modern morality, they can hardly be blamed. But this reaction, which is only that of a section, is in its nature a reaction of the young and as such I do not think it will last. I know it is the cant phrase of the old rationalists that their reason prevents a return to the Faith, but it is false: it is no longer reason but rather passion.

This may sound a sweeping statement, but if it be examined it will be found not unjust, and certainly not unsympathetic. Nothing is

---

[47] Futurism, whose major proponent was the Italian Filippo Marinetti (1876–1944), was an avant-garde artistic and literary movement that arose just before World War I. It celebrated dynamism, violence and the machine age.

more notable if we really study the character-
istics of the rising generation than the fact that
they are *not* acting upon any exact and definite philosophy, such as those which have made
the revolutions of the past. If they are anarchical, they are not anarchist. The dogmatic
anarchism of the middle of the nineteenth century is not the creed they hold, or even the
excuse they offer. They have a considerable
negative revolt against religion, a negative revolt
against negative morality. They have a feeling,
which is not unreasonable, that to commit
themselves to the Catholic citizenship is to take
responsibilities that continually act as restraints.
But they do not maintain anything like a contrary system of spiritual citizenship, or moral
responsibility. For instance, it is perfectly natural that they should want to act naturally. But
they do not want to act naturally according to
any intellectual theory of the reliability of
Nature. On the contrary, their young and bril-
liant literary representatives are very prone to
press upon us the crudity and cruelty of Nature.
That is the moral of Mr. Aldous Huxley, and
of many others. State to them any of the con-
sistent theories of the supreme claim of Nature

upon us, such as the pantheistic idea of God in all natural things; or the Nietzschean theory that nature is evolving something with superior claims to our own; or any other definable defence of the natural process itself, and they will almost certainly reject it as something unproved or exploded. They do not want to have an exact imitation of the laws of the physical universe; they want to have their own way, a much more intelligible desire. But the result is that they are, after all, at a disadvantage in face of those other young people who have satisfied their reason by a scheme that makes the universe reasonable.

For that is the very simple explanation of the affair. In so far as there is really a secession among the young, it is but a part of the same process as that conversion of the young, of which I wrote in the first chapter. The rising generation sees the real issue; and those who are ready for it rally, and those who are not ready for it scatter. But there can be but one end to a war between a solid and a scattered army. It is not a controversy between two philosophies, as was the Catholic and the Calvinist, or the Catholic and the Materialist. It is a controversy between philosophers and philanderers. I do not say it in contempt; I have much more sympathy with the person who leaves the Church for a love-affair than with one who leaves it for a long-winded German theory to prove that God is evil or that children are a sort of morbid monkey. But the very laws of life are against the endurance of a revolt that rests on nothing but natural passion; it is bound to change in its proportion with the coming of experience; and, at the worst, it will become a battle between bad Catholics and good Catholics, with the great dome over all.